WIDE OPEN
WORKSPACE

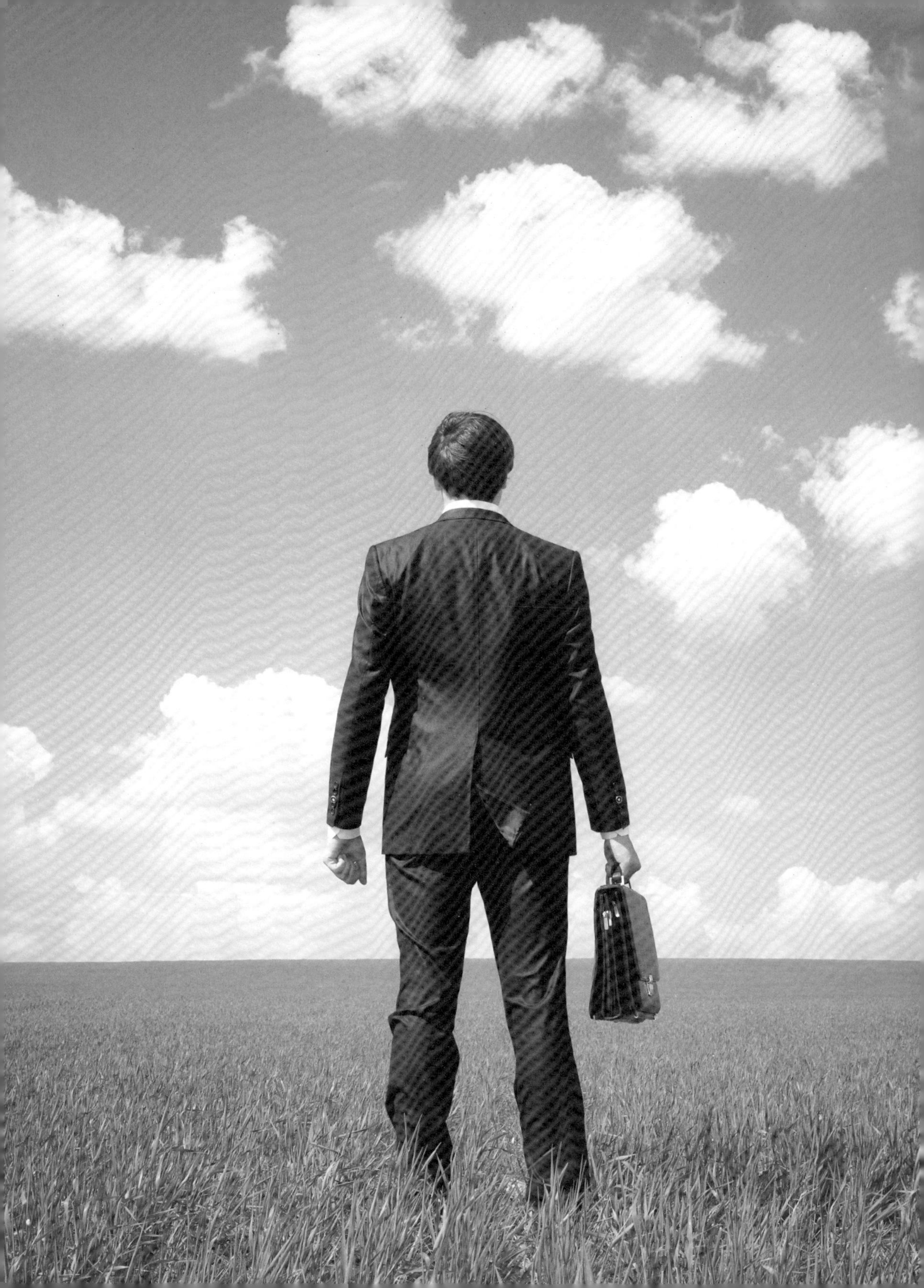

WIDE OPEN WORKSPACE

TRAILBLAZING SOLUTIONS FOR TOMORROW'S WORKFORCE

ELIZABETH DUKES + DON TRAWEEK

WCT
PUBLISHING

Seabrook, Texas

Copyright © 2014 by Elizabeth Dukes and Don Traweek. All rights reserved.

No part of this book may be reproduced or transmitted in any form or by any means, graphic, electronic, or mechanical, including photocopying, recording, taping or by any information storage or retrieval system, without the permission in writing from the publisher.

For more information, contact:
WCT Publishing
2022 Lakeside Landing
Seabrook, Texas 77586
www.WideOpenWorkspace.com

Publisher's Cataloging-in-Publication data

Dukes, Elizabeth.
   Wide open workspace : trailblazing solutions for tomorrow's workforce / Elizabeth Dukes and Don Traweek.
   p. cm.
   ISBN 978-0-615-97028-8
   Includes bibliographical references and index.

   1. Facility management. 2. Office management. 3. Corporations --Management. 4. Real estate management. 5. Building management. 6. Cowboys --West (U.S.) --History. 7. Texas --History. I. Traweek, Don. II. Title.

HD1394 .D85 2014
658.2 --dc23   2014933468

Book concept and strategy by TwinEngine | www.twinengine.com
Book production consulting by Books by Brookes | www.booksbybrookes.com
Book and cover design by *the*BookDesigners | www.thebookdesigners.com

Stock Photography Credits:
©Fotosearch.com: ©OJO Images pp. 7, 111, 129;
©Uppercut Images p. 9; ©Fotosearch p. 103

©Gettyimages.com: ©Hero Images p. 27; ©Lise Gagne p. 32;
©Johnny Greig p. 63; ©Anton Ovcharenko p. 73

©Shutterstock.com: pp. ii, viii, 16, 21, 24, 28, 32, 36,
50, 64, 79, 80, 92, 94, 106, 120, 134, 140

©iStockPhoto.com: p. 12

Printed in the United States of America

We would like to dedicate this book to
all the unsung heroes of the back office—
those who make sure the doors are open,
the lights are on, the air is pleasant,
and the coffee is brewing.

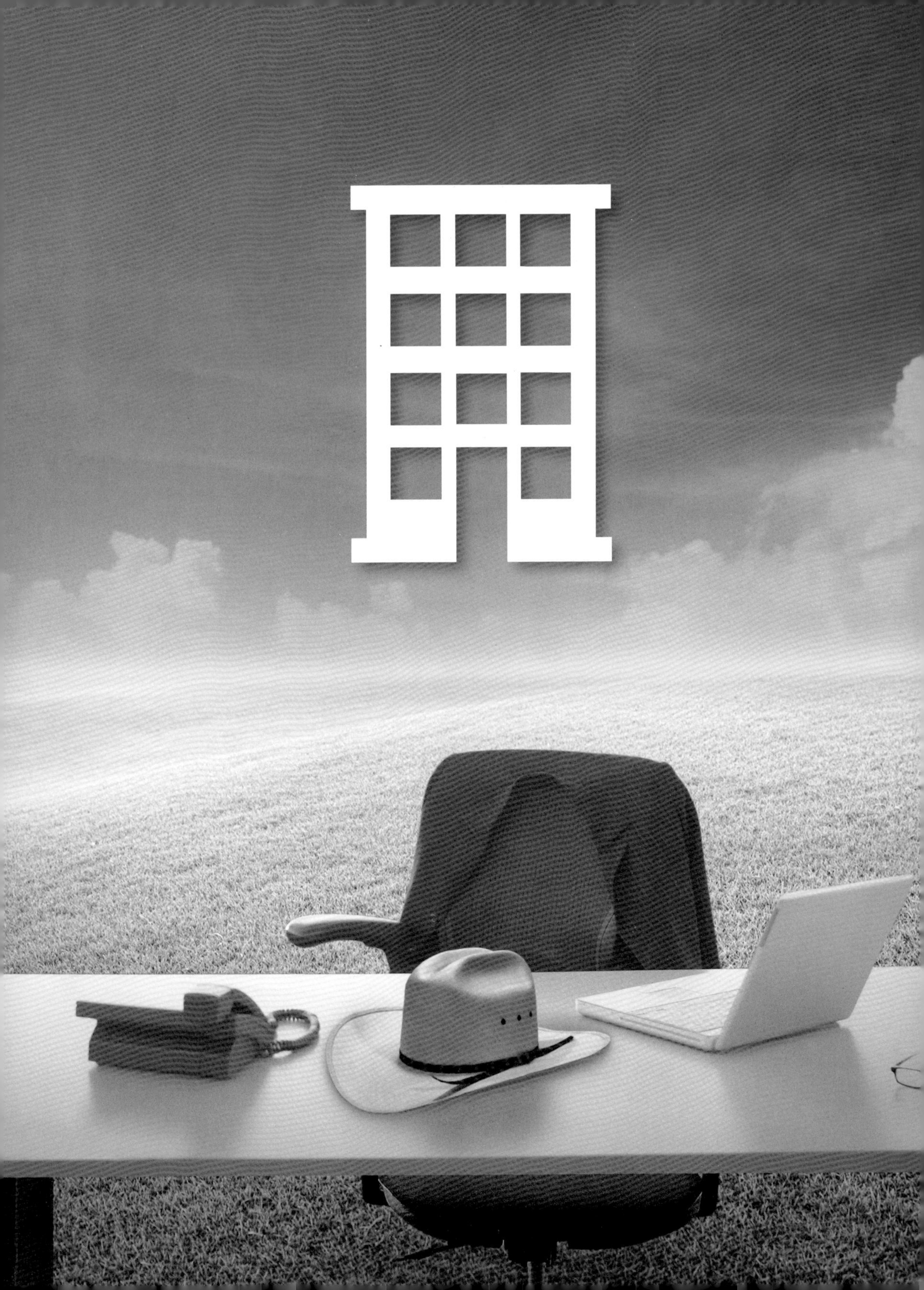

CONTENTS

AN INVITATION TO RIDE 1

CODE #1: Cowboys Blaze New Trails 17

CODE #2: Cowboys Get Together for the Roundup 37

CODE #3: Cowboys Have Ten-Gallon Courage to Do What Needs to Be Done ... 51

CODE #4: Cowboys Take Pride in Their Chores 65

CODE #5: Cowboys Keep an Eye Out for What Works 81

CODE #6: A Cowboy's Word Is as Good as Gold 95

CODE #7: Cowboys Share around the Campfire 107

CODE #8: Cowboys Ride for the Brand 121

NEW FRONTIERS AWAIT 135

Acknowledgments 139
Bibliography 141
Index 145

RIDE!

AN INVITATION TO RIDE

THE WORKPLACE IS changing dramatically and at a fearsome pace. Where and how people work are being transformed. Technology-fluent workers, the imperative for business collaboration, "paperless" initiatives, smart buildings, the cloud, and other mobility enablers—these trends and more are turning facilities management on its head.

At the same time, many of the traditional functions—the nuts and bolts that keep an enterprise operating smoothly—must still be performed, around the clock, day after day. Most people have little notion of what it takes to run a building, let alone a whole host of real estate properties. To top it off, companies seeking lower expenses look to those who manage their real estate to save money. After all, space (whether it is a rented office or a complex of company-owned buildings) represents the second highest operating cost in most companies, right behind payroll.

The constant search for better performance and utilization of real estate assets is just one of the reasons behind the dramatic changes. Other forces are evolving technology, corporate objectives to "go green," and the skills and expectations of the young talent that is entering the workforce. In forward-looking companies, workers are not held in by walls or tethered to a specific physical location. Mobility within the corporate setting is enhancing collaboration, innovation, and creativity. Enabled by technology to work anywhere and anytime, employees are more productive and can enjoy more balanced lives.

At iOffice, our vision of the future of facilities management is something we call "Wide Open Workspace" (WOW). WOW is not a passing phase, but a transformation that is already touching companies around the globe.

ENABLED BY TECHNOLOGY TO WORK ANYWHERE AND ANYTIME, EMPLOYEES ARE MORE PRODUCTIVE AND CAN ENJOY MORE BALANCED LIVES.

Companies that hope to compete for the best talent, develop innovative products and services, and excel in customer relationships are embracing the new possibilities. WOW is a movement that supports superior performance of not just the real estate assets, but the business as a whole. The people who are driving this dramatic shift are a group we refer to as Workspace Cowboys. This book is about them and dedicated to those who want to join them in shaping workspaces that will enable and empower the workforce, wherever it may roam.

iOFFICE AND THE WORKSPACE CHALLENGE

iOffice is in the thick of this upheaval. We compete in an industry called integrated workplace management services. We think of ourselves as partners who provide simple, flexible tools to help Facilities Managers get their jobs done. Our software helps streamline a whole host of tasks. For example, iOffice can help the Facilities Team

- maintain and repair facilities in a timely, proactive manner;
- monitor supplies to have what is needed without excess inventory;
- execute efficient moves with minimal downtime;
- reserve conference rooms and track visitors to support collaboration;
- manage mail, copying, and printing; and
- help optimize the utilization of space, furniture, and equipment, with a positive impact on the bottom line.

We recognize that different organizations are at different stages in the evolution of their workspaces. Each is unique, and some may never change from a traditional structure. Nonetheless, our commitment is to provide software that helps manage a traditional office environment *and* solutions to manage in the "new age" of work. We want you to run your business in the most effective manner for your specific needs, no matter where you are on the spectrum—from closed offices to completely open spaces.

iOffice is the name of our company and it is also the name of our product. The iOffice platform is a cloud-based, single point of access with multiple functions and support tools. In this book, when we are referring to our software solutions, we will use the phrase *iOffice platform*. Otherwise, *iOffice* will refer to our company and our team of professionals.

Working with our customers to manage and reshape their work worlds, we are seeing firsthand the enormous challenges—and bold moves to overcome them. Being Texas based, we recognize certain parallels between some of our customers and the cowboys who shaped the American West. Like the cowboys of old, Facilities Managers are finding new paths through the Wide Open Workspace of the Digital Age. Cowboys were the original entrepreneurs and innovators of the Old West. At iOffice, we are proud to call ourselves Workspace Cowboys. We, too, are entrepreneurs, working with other business people who are looking toward the future, always wondering what's beyond the next mountain.

COWBOYS AS AN INSPIRATION

The open range serves as an excellent metaphor for today's modern workspace—unbounded, uncharted to a large extent, and full of opportunities. Likewise, the cowboy is an excellent metaphor for the workspace professional. The cowboy has long been a symbol of the great frontier as well as a person associated with honor, respect, and pride. The best of the breed were courageous, adventurous, and heroic, venturing out into the open plains with little more than a horse and a ten-gallon hat. Buffalo Bill and Wild Bill

Hickok, two of the most notable cowboys in the Old West, had appetites for discovery and invention while holding strong reputations as a scout and a lawman, respectively. Cowboys lived a unique lifestyle that was influenced by their surroundings; they slept in the fields, looking into the clear sky above, and envisioned what adventures lay ahead.

AT iOFFICE, OUR VISION OF THE FUTURE OF FACILITIES MANAGEMENT IS SOMETHING WE CALL "WIDE OPEN WORKSPACE" (WOW). WOW IS NOT A PASSING PHASE, BUT A TRANSFORMATION THAT IS ALREADY TOUCHING COMPANIES AROUND THE GLOBE.

As the cowboys of the Old West explored the wide open spaces, they also had responsibilities. The role of the cowboy developed from the need to move cattle from one location to the next. Large herds of cattle managed by teams of cowboys traveled the Chisholm Trail from Texas to Kansas. The journey was nothing glamorous, but for the cowboy it was a way of life and the way he earned his wages. As they traveled the open plains, the cowboys were free to ride the great frontier but they had to be very attentive to their herd. They took great care and initiative in fulfilling their first responsibility—looking after the cattle.

WHO IS THE WORKSPACE COWBOY?

Before answering this question, let's examine the responsibilities of the people who are stewards of the workplace. Perhaps you are one yourself.

Whatever your title may be (they vary dramatically across organizations), you have multiple tasks. You have basic blocking and tackling, everyday requests to which you must respond—demands from Human Resources (HR), demands from Information Technology (IT), demands from the executive leadership, and demands from the workforce.

WE WANT YOU TO RUN YOUR BUSINESS IN THE MOST EFFECTIVE MANNER FOR YOUR SPECIFIC NEEDS, NO MATTER WHERE YOU ARE ON THE SPECTRUM—FROM CLOSED OFFICES TO COMPLETELY OPEN SPACES.

Most Facilities Managers have a broad range of fundamental responsibilities that start with the physical space and what's in it. For example, when a new hire arrives, the Facilities Team coordinates with other areas to be sure things are in place so that the new recruit can do his or her job. They work with IT to make sure that a computer is set up; they make sure there is a desk and a chair to sit in and a phone with a dial tone. When a team or department moves, a whole herd needs tending!

Facilities Teams also deliver the services that maintain the physical plant and ensure that employees have what they need to do their jobs—from pens and pencils to Voice-over-Internet-Protocol phone capabilities. They're often responsible for the reception area and the first impressions visitors have of the company. They coordinate meeting spaces, making sure the rooms are configured correctly and have the right audiovisual support. Typically, they are responsible for the office equipment: the printers

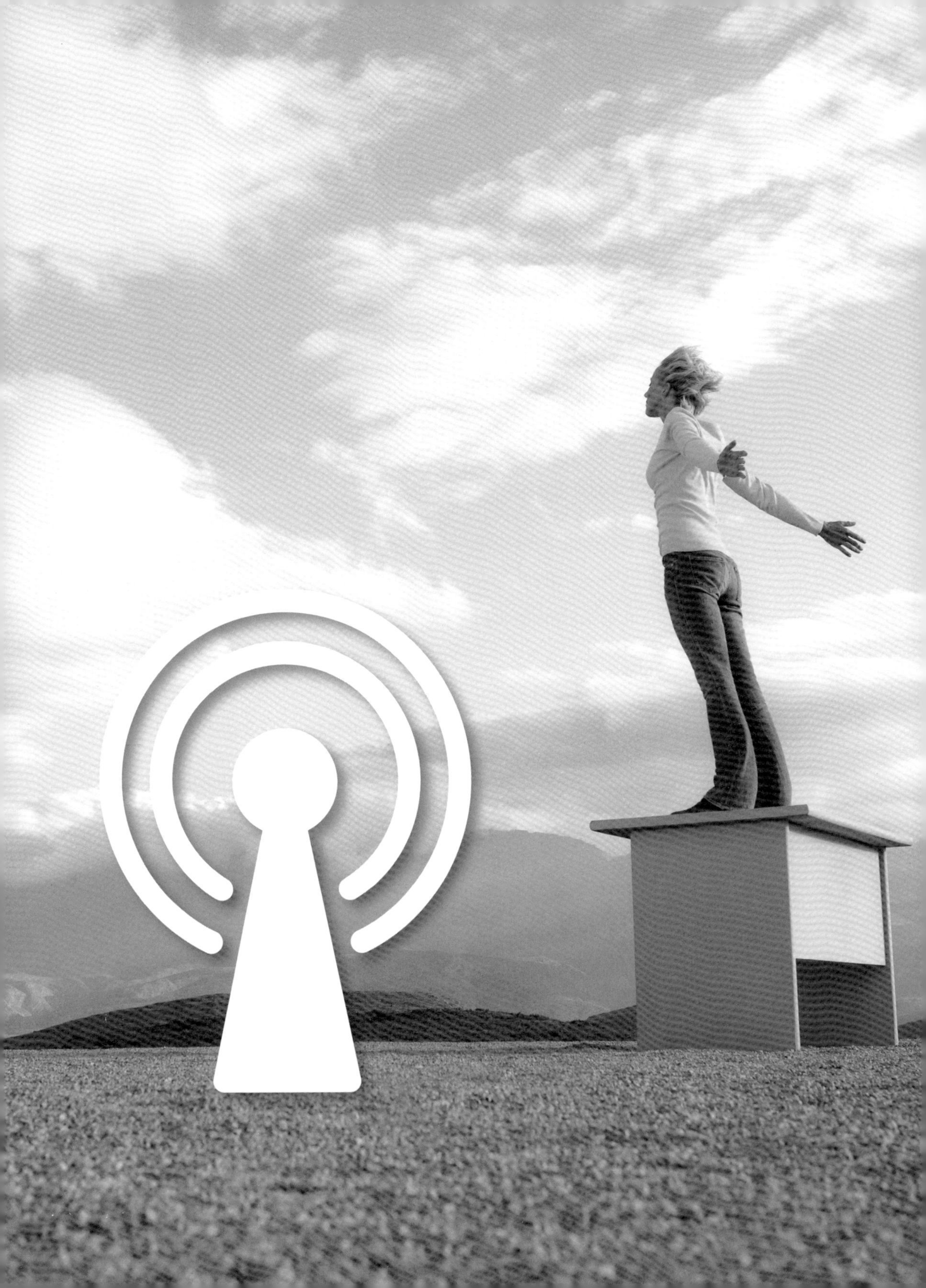

and MFPs (multifunctional printers), coffee machines, fire extinguishers, and life safety equipment. Sometimes they are responsible for all the office services: incoming mail and package delivery, centralized printing center, or perhaps the file room.

More recent responsibilities include corporate green initiatives—the recycling programs, clean products for building maintenance, and LEED* certifications. In addition to implementing these programs, they monitor and measure to ensure that the enterprise is a good corporate citizen. In a small business, it could be something as simple as getting, labeling, and emptying the buckets for paper recycling. In a large corporation, it could be overseeing construction of a LEED building complex.

If the space is leased, another entity may manage the building and maintain the utility systems, pest control, or landscaping. However, as the tenant's representative, the Facilities Manager must make sure that the lease agreements are executed properly. No one wants to be overcharged or have their lease expire! Another task is the continuous evaluation of whether the space is the right fit for the organization. The Facilities Manager is likely to lead the efforts to find and recommend a new location or explore real estate investments to accommodate growth.

These multifaceted players fall at many levels in company hierarchies, from supervisor to middle manager to senior executive. They carry many titles, ranging from Manager of Facilities Services to Director of Global Corporate Real

---

* LEED = Leadership in Energy and Environmental Design

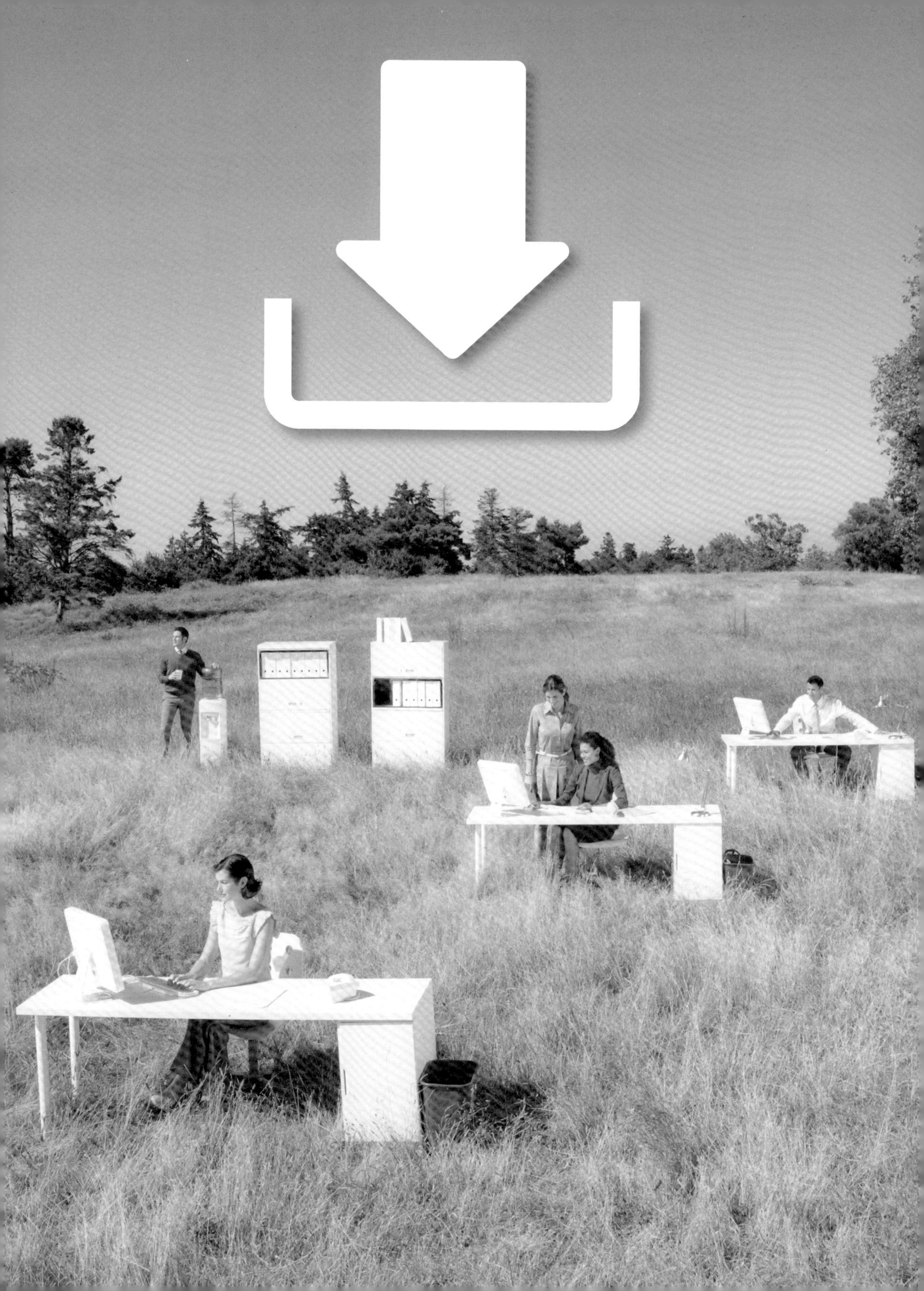

Estate to Chief Operating Officer (COO). As workspace evolves, so do the titles. At Google, these responsibilities belong to the Chief of Workplace.

Your title, and your roles, may be unique. But no matter what you are called, we'll wager that you have many, many tasks. You're doing all the basic blocking and tackling . . . and chances are your role is changing.

YOUR TITLE, AND YOUR ROLES, MAY BE UNIQUE. BUT NO MATTER WHAT YOU ARE CALLED, WE'LL WAGER THAT YOU HAVE MANY, MANY TASKS. YOU'RE DOING ALL THE BASIC BLOCKING AND TACKLING . . . AND CHANCES ARE YOUR ROLE IS CHANGING.

The duties of the Facilities Manager are expanding. The job now includes creating a workplace that is attractive to the workforce, an environment that engenders collaboration and raises productivity. This is especially true in industries that compete for "knowledge workers," but it also applies to all kinds of organizations. Facilities Managers not only want to attract and retain workers, they also must be good stewards of real estate that is economically viable for the organization. It is difficult to do all that is expected with just spreadsheets and voicemail. Planning, decision-making, and implementation of workspace activities across this wide spectrum require new skills and the help of the right technology.

If you embrace the tools and mindset of a Workspace Cowboy, you will have opportunities to bring new data, new ideas, and new approaches to your organization. Your sphere of influence will grow. You will affect the results of the entire organization. You will no longer be in charge of just the physical plant, but a partner in the transformation of your company's way of working. You will be taking care of your herd whether it is home or away, helping to keep a top-notch workforce performing at its peak.

Let us add an important note here. Our notion of the Workspace Cowboy is gender neutral. Many outstanding Facilities Managers are women. The cowboy spirit, the courage to forge new trails in new frontiers, is alive and well in both women and men alike. In this book, the term *cowboy* is used in an inclusive sense, embracing cowgirls and cowboys and the special skills they exercise to get their jobs done.

THE COWBOY CODE

John Wayne, one of the greatest American film and television actors of the 20th century, once said, "A man's got to have a code, a creed to live by." He believed that every person should be guided by a particular code of honor and loyalty. Those traits are still seen in some of the great entrepreneurs and business executives in the modern economy. A business that is guided by a clear mission and dedicated to the needs of its employees and clients has a much better chance of being successful than one without compelling values.

Cowboys lived and worked by a code, and so do Workspace Cowboys. Drawing from our experience with our customers and our Texas heritage, we have identified eight codes—behaviors from another time when new horizons provided opportunity. We have seen these codes played

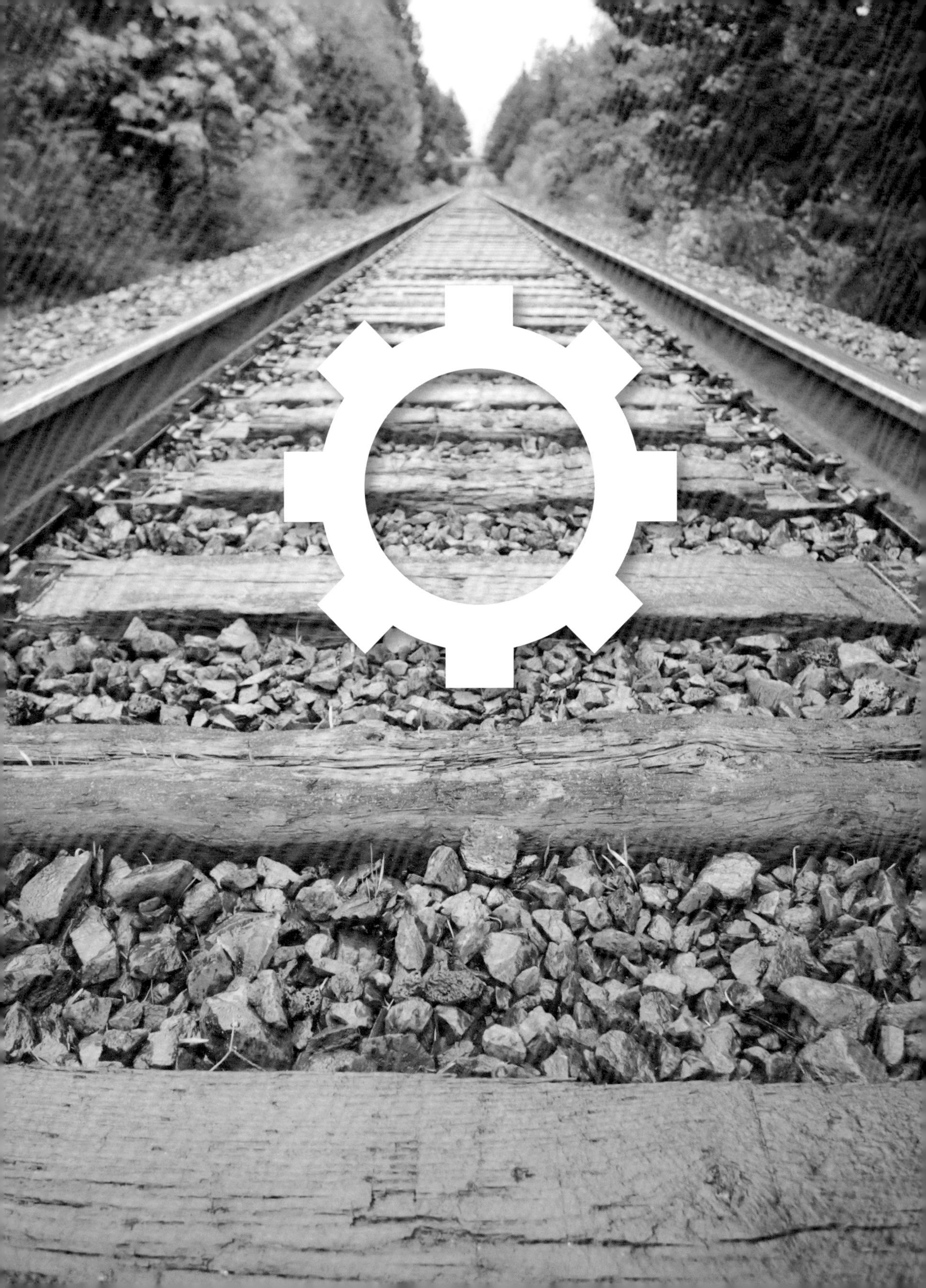

AN INVITATION TO RIDE

out by the leaders of the facilities profession and believe they can guide us all through the uncharted workplace territory that lies ahead.

JOHN WAYNE ONCE SAID, "A MAN'S GOT TO HAVE A CODE, A CREED TO LIVE BY."

These eight codes are not only the chapters of this book, but also the creed that guides iOffice as we work with our customers.

1. Cowboys blaze new trails.
2. Cowboys get together for the roundup.
3. Cowboys have ten-gallon courage to do what needs to be done.
4. Cowboys take pride in their chores.
5. Cowboys keep an eye out for what works.
6. A cowboy's word is as good as gold.
7. Cowboys share around the campfire.
8. Cowboys ride for the brand.

We will illustrate the cowboy codes with real examples that we have witnessed in our professional activities. Many of these come from our customers, an extremely valuable source of past learning and insight about what might lie ahead. To preserve confidentiality, we do not mention the companies by name, but we do indicate the sector they represent. These examples encompass healthcare, financial services, retail, natural resources, higher education, and business solutions. In talking about our customers, we will refer to the individuals with whom we have worked by the generic title *Corporate & Facilities Services Representatives*. In addition, we will use the terms *Facilities Manager* and *Facilities Team* to cover a very diverse group of professionals in these organizations.

When writing this book, we reached out to some of our customers to ask for their views about the evolution of the work environment. Their perspectives are presented in sidebars labeled "Voice of the Customer." We thank them anonymously for their generous "sharing around the campfire."

IF YOU EMBRACE THE TOOLS AND MINDSET OF A WORKSPACE COWBOY, YOU WILL HAVE OPPORTUNITIES TO BRING NEW DATA, NEW IDEAS, AND NEW APPROACHES TO YOUR ORGANIZATION.

Along the way, we will share some other stories—of Texas history, cowboy heritage, and business success. The iOffice team has been inspired by these pioneers who have blazed new trails. As Workspace Cowboys at iOffice, we strive to do the same in the Wide Open Workspace. We hope we will see you on the trail.

VOICE OF THE CUSTOMER

WORKSPACE EVOLUTION

We spoke to some of our trailblazing customers from diverse industries to get their views about what might lie around the bend. Here are some of the trends they see shaping the new workspace.

FORCES DRIVING CHANGE. "The workplace is changing at a rapid pace. Two forces are driving the change: 1) the expectations of employees and 2) companies looking to improve economics around developing and maintaining space."

GENERATIONAL SHIFT. "There is a generational workforce change that we're seeing across the world. It *is* across the world, not only here in the United States. As workers get younger and younger and younger (i.e., the Millennials), they are a disruptive force. They have changed the way people view a piece of paper. Now an iPad emulates a piece of paper. Youngsters are accessing and placing documents directly in the cloud. They are not printing those documents and placing them in file folders and cabinets."

CORPORATE CITIZENSHIP. "Many employees working for Fortune 500 companies are very interested in being part of an organization that is environmentally responsible, community driven, and that promotes employee wellness. Company commitment is evident from actions such as robust recycling/composting programs, open space plans with lots of natural light, LEED certifications, company-sponsored fitness programs, support of local charities, and support of our nation's military."

FOCUS ON COLLABORATION. "Today the emphasis is on collaboration, open spaces, lots of natural light, color, mobility, and amenities. This affects our strategy in real estate and our operations for facilities management. The entire organization needs to be nimble."

SMALLER FOOTPRINT AND SMALLER EXPENDITURES. "Leaders in real estate and specifically in facilities management recognize opportunities to leverage new concepts to create more efficient workspaces in order to reduce the real estate footprint and overall spend. This includes promoting worker mobility and investing in technology to improve the performance of the talent base. While the corporation increases productivity and reduces the cost of hosting workers, employees can be more productive and experience better work/life balance."

BLAZE

CODE #1: COWBOYS BLAZE NEW TRAILS

BLAZING NEW TRAILS creates opportunities for those who dare to venture into the unknown. Facilities management as a discipline is facing challenges, uncertainties, and uncharted terrain. The present upheaval in the work environment is being felt to different degrees in different industries. Many companies still have traditional office configurations. However, we believe that every high-performing enterprise has or will need to make changes in where and how their employees work if they want to remain competitive. That makes it imperative for the Facilities Team to "blaze new trails"—to find new ways of doing things and to get others to join them in that quest.

WE BELIEVE THAT EVERY HIGH-PERFORMING ENTERPRISE HAS OR WILL NEED TO MAKE CHANGES IN WHERE AND HOW THEIR EMPLOYEES WORK IF THEY WANT TO REMAIN COMPETITIVE.

Cowboys have a track record of trailblazing that provides some useful lessons. The first cattle arrived in Texas in the 15th century with Spanish explorers, but for decades the herds ran wild, feeding off the prairie grass. The Spanish found Texas largely inhospitable and never took a serious interest in developing a colony there. Their primary interest was military, to discourage other European countries from sniffing around for potential colonies.

ALTHOUGH BARBED WIRE AND RAILROADS EVENTUALLY BROUGHT AN END TO THOSE ONCE INNOVATIVE CATTLE DRIVES, THE NOTION OF BLAZING TRAILS HAS BEEN EMBEDDED IN THE TEXAS BUSINESS CULTURE EVER SINCE.

By the end of the Civil War, the cattle numbered in the millions. Because people could easily bring home their own beef, the cows weren't worth much—on the Texas range. However, a few smart cowboys realized that if the cattle were moved up north, they would be worth a fortune. The challenge was to get the cattle from Texas to Chicago, where they would fetch a handsome sum.

The prospect of wealth was tantalizing, even for the rawest dude. Most free-range cattle were unbranded. With the help of a few pals, you could round up several hundred head, brand them, and move them to railheads in Kansas—if you had a trail! Cowboys rose to the challenge. Some cowboys began to "head 'em up, move 'em out," forging routes through untamed territory. Others looked around and found a "resource" that they could turn to their use—the broad, flat trail that Jesse Chisholm had blazed for heavy merchant wagons. Thus, some cowboys carved out new paths, while others converted one that was created for a different purpose. Either way, they saw a way to extract value from the assets at hand, even though it meant finding their way across some pretty rough terrain.

Although barbed wire and railroads eventually brought an end to those once innovative cattle drives, the notion of blazing trails has been embedded in the Texas business culture ever since. Being willing to set out in a new direction, even if it was a rough ride, is a trait that cowboys and successful businessmen share. Three quick examples come to mind: the "roughnecks" who built the oil business; the unorthodox founders of Southwest Airlines, who based their planes in small satellite airports rather than in the overcrowded major hubs; and Michael Dell, who built computers to order for fellow students at the University of Texas.

TRAILBLAZING IN THE WORKSPACE ARENA

Now let's look at some recent trailblazing in the facilities management arena. One of the most dramatic trends affecting the work environment today is the transition to flexible work environments, referred to as *flexspace*. The term *Flexspace* was coined by Sabre Holdings, a company that provides technology-based services to the travel industry.*

---

* In 2012, Sabre Holdings published a detailed case that is publicly available: "Sustainable Business Transformation through Workspace Innovation." Filled with valuable details, it is recommended reading for any executive or manager who wants to understand the impact workspace can have on business performance. We will talk more about Sabre and its program when we explore Code #8: Cowboys Ride for the Brand.

Nowadays, *flexspace* is a term widely used to describe reconfigurations of corporate offices that use modern technology and design concepts to achieve higher space utilization and increase team collaboration.

Traditionally, the office mindset was that each worker had an assigned space that stayed constant from day to day. The focus was on the physical space rather than on the type of work or the amount of time the person was actually at his or her desk. For example, many salespeople and account managers are in the field with their customers more than half the time. People in some functions and roles spend many days in meetings or training sessions, leaving their desks vacant for several days running, not to mention vacancies during vacation weeks. Flexspace thinking examines the actual utilization of desk space and redesigns around the principle of sharing space. By adapting to the reality of a mobile workforce and being flexible about where people sit, an organization may, for instance, need 25 spaces instead of 50 dedicated offices. That allows for a dramatic reduction in facilities costs.

BY ADAPTING TO THE REALITY OF A MOBILE WORKFORCE AND BEING FLEXIBLE ABOUT WHERE PEOPLE SIT, AN ORGANIZATION MAY, FOR INSTANCE, NEED 25 SPACES INSTEAD OF 50 DEDICATED OFFICES. THAT ALLOWS FOR A DRAMATIC REDUCTION IN FACILITIES COSTS.

Some companies embraced this concept long ago. Accounting firms, for example, have used "hoteling" to give professionals a temporary office at their home office, a place accountants go infrequently if they are assigned to work on

CONTEMPORARY BIZ

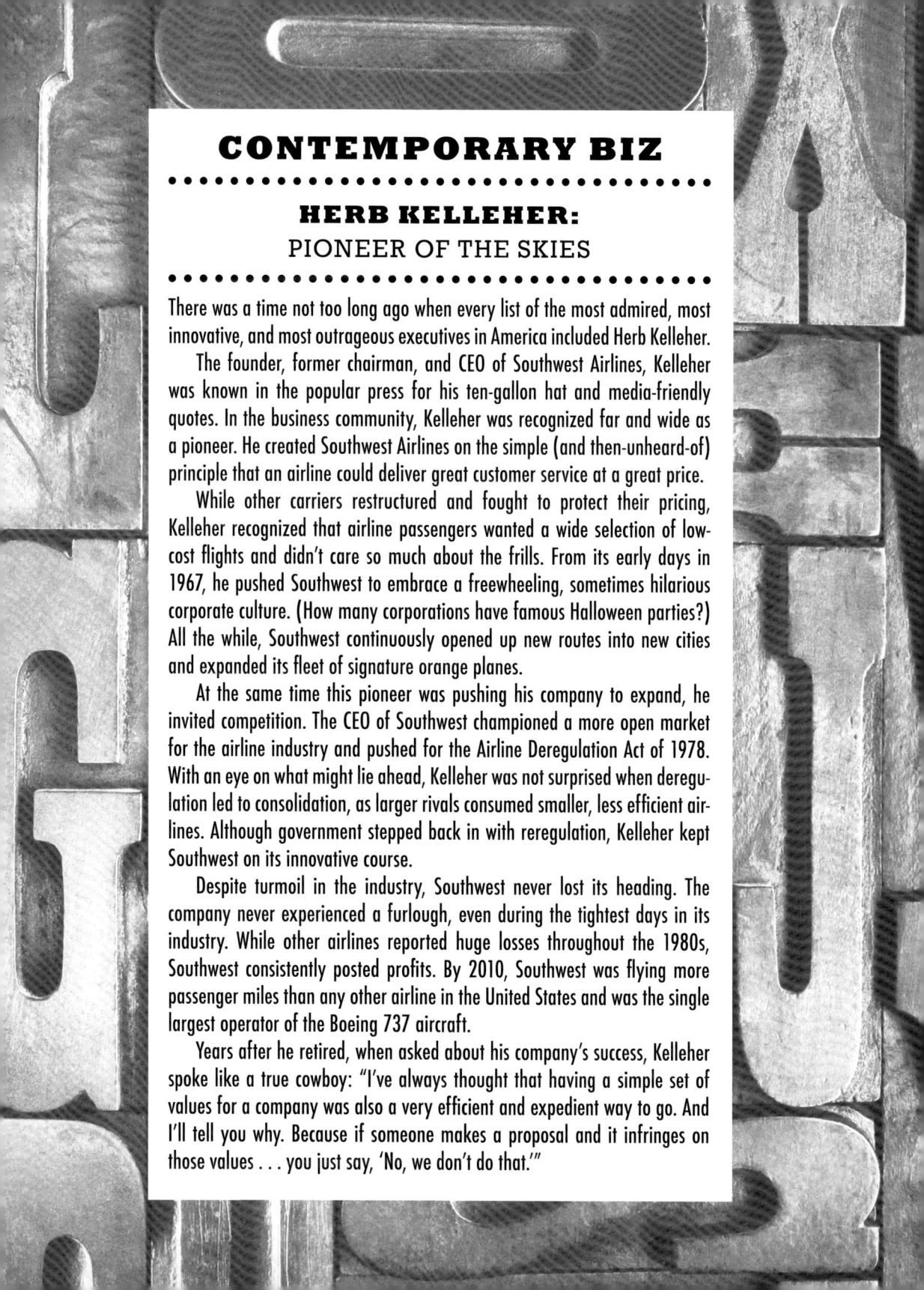

HERB KELLEHER:
PIONEER OF THE SKIES

There was a time not too long ago when every list of the most admired, most innovative, and most outrageous executives in America included Herb Kelleher.

The founder, former chairman, and CEO of Southwest Airlines, Kelleher was known in the popular press for his ten-gallon hat and media-friendly quotes. In the business community, Kelleher was recognized far and wide as a pioneer. He created Southwest Airlines on the simple (and then-unheard-of) principle that an airline could deliver great customer service at a great price.

While other carriers restructured and fought to protect their pricing, Kelleher recognized that airline passengers wanted a wide selection of low-cost flights and didn't care so much about the frills. From its early days in 1967, he pushed Southwest to embrace a freewheeling, sometimes hilarious corporate culture. (How many corporations have famous Halloween parties?) All the while, Southwest continuously opened up new routes into new cities and expanded its fleet of signature orange planes.

At the same time this pioneer was pushing his company to expand, he invited competition. The CEO of Southwest championed a more open market for the airline industry and pushed for the Airline Deregulation Act of 1978. With an eye on what might lie ahead, Kelleher was not surprised when deregulation led to consolidation, as larger rivals consumed smaller, less efficient airlines. Although government stepped back in with reregulation, Kelleher kept Southwest on its innovative course.

Despite turmoil in the industry, Southwest never lost its heading. The company never experienced a furlough, even during the tightest days in its industry. While other airlines reported huge losses throughout the 1980s, Southwest consistently posted profits. By 2010, Southwest was flying more passenger miles than any other airline in the United States and was the single largest operator of the Boeing 737 aircraft.

Years after he retired, when asked about his company's success, Kelleher spoke like a true cowboy: "I've always thought that having a simple set of values for a company was also a very efficient and expedient way to go. And I'll tell you why. Because if someone makes a proposal and it infringes on those values . . . you just say, 'No, we don't do that.'"

site for billable clients. Another example is engineers, who may have a physical space assigned at their customer location rather than at their company's base of operations. The idea of sharing space is not new; however, its use in companies for their non-traveling workforce or their senior executives is! Let's look at a couple of other examples of companies that have blazed trails in the flexspace arena. (As mentioned in the introduction of this book, these are real company experiences that have been disguised to protect the confidentiality of our customers.)

iOffice works with a healthcare network that is a recognized pioneer in the medical field and a trailblazer in promoting worker mobility and variable workspace. As an employee of this network, if you work away from the office for 50 percent or more of the time, your office goes into the pool to be used by other employees during your absence.

COWBOYS LIVED AND WORKED BY A CODE, AND SO DO WORKSPACE COWBOYS.

Of course, not everyone is ready to "ride the trail" of mobility and flexspace; some department heads want their people in the office, in assigned spaces. A change of this magnitude requires an effective leader with focus on the details. It also requires significant buy-in from senior management and line leaders to promote the change and place it in a positive light. The Corporate & Facilities Services Representative from this healthcare network had this to say about the human side of trailblazing with flexspace.

> *Well-coordinated change management processes with plenty of communication pre-launch, launch, and post-launch are highly important. Training folks how to adapt to new work philosophies and environments is also important. Taking the necessary time to address concerns is one of the keys to long-term success of any project that impacts individual workers.*

He went on to describe what to expect during such a transition.

> *Most employees realize the benefits of creating flex-space to improve space utilization. They also like the idea of being mobile; however, many still prefer to have a place to call "home." Those new to the workforce are much more adaptable than those who have been working in standard office environments for long periods of time. The number of folks who can leave behind the notion that you have to be at your desk or at a specific desk in order to truly work is increasing. Those who readily embrace technology adapt easily as well.*

This example illustrates that it is one thing to blaze a trail; it is another to get the herd to move in the direction you want. By understanding the different segments of the workforce and their attitudes, this Workspace Cowboy tailored his change management and communication strategy to achieve the least resistance. For this healthcare network, this huge change is slowly gaining ground as new sites are brought on-line and existing sites are renovated. No one said trailblazing is easy.

COWBOY HISTORY

JESSE CHISHOLM:
BLAZING THE CHISHOLM TRAIL

Talk about wide open spaces . . . Jesse Chisholm was an expert in navigating the unknown, whether that meant laying down the trail that bore his name or peacefully moving between the sometimes hostile cultures that populated the Texas grasslands at the beginning of the 19th century.

Chisholm was actually born in Tennessee, sometime around 1806, to a Scottish father and a Cherokee mother. From his earliest days in the raw western country, Chisholm straddled multiple worlds. Naturally, he became a trader, fluent in 14 dialects, a man who could negotiate with the Native American tribes throughout Oklahoma and Texas just as well as he could sell goods and trade with the white Americans who were never far behind.

In the early part of his career, Chisholm was chiefly known for setting up trading posts throughout southern Oklahoma, then foraying into the wild Texas countryside as an interpreter and guide. Both sides—Native American and white alike—recognized that Chisholm was a man of character who could be trusted in his business dealings. This is perhaps why Sam Houston, the first president of Texas, called upon Chisholm to contact the prairie Indians in the western part of the state and open talks between the tribes and the state government.

While this work was important, it's his trailblazing that earned Chisholm lasting fame. As he traveled through the wild lands, navigating between Native Americans, Mexicans, and Americans, Chisholm built a series of trading posts that stretched from Texas up to the big rail yards in Kansas City. Known as the Chisholm Trail, this is the path cowboys used to move cattle herds up from their grazing territory to the stockyards.

It would be hard to underestimate the importance of trails like this to the rapid colonization of Texas. Back then, beef on the hoof grazed in the open prairie lands, where grass and water were plentiful. But there wasn't much of a market for beef in Texas—not enough people lived there, and there were lots of cows. Instead, the big markets for beef were in the teeming cities back east, where beef cattle could fetch ten times the price it commanded in Texas. The problem, of course, was getting the beef from the Texas prairie to the New York butcher.

And that's really where Chisholm's trailblazing came in. By laying down the best route, he gave generations of cowboys a means to move herds of Longhorn cattle to the rail terminals that connected the East Coast to the frontier like so many arteries. The trail that bore his name was the heart and soul of the cowboy ethos and an early example of entrepreneurship in Texas.

W**ORKFORCE MOBILITY IS** not the only factor that leads companies to reconfigure their space. A few years ago, an iOffice customer in the financial services industry began a very thoughtful, process-oriented initiative to develop a workplace strategy. After a lot of study, the company is currently in the midst of a major renovation to convert a 20-year-old "high-cube farm" environment into something more contemporary, innovative, and supportive of the company's current work style and culture.

The Project Manager of this process said, *"We are low-mobility when it comes to teleworking, so we don't have a lot of work-from-home folks, but we are very mobile within the workplace. That has helped shape our workplace."* To support that internal mobility, the renovation will more than double the amount of collaborative space (from 10–15 percent to about 40 percent) while reducing the space per workseat (from 180 to 170 square feet).

The change encompassed more than the physical move. *"You could walk into the facility and have no idea that you were in our company offices. It could be any company in the USA. So, we wanted the space to feel like our brand. When people walk into our space, we want them to feel like they are someplace special. So we chose colors that reflect our brand. We chose workstations with much lower cube walls, a lot of glass, and a lot of natural light coming into the space."*

The company worked hard to make people more comfortable and more engaged with the new space, with attention to daylight and views. Although the result has been overwhelmingly positive, for some people change is hard. Some people liked the high walls and the old-fashioned work environment. Recognizing this challenge, the company started to manage change very early with a change management team and a formal change process. While the strategy was being defined, focus groups and surveys of employees and managers solicited input. Furniture mockups and visual sessions engaged the workforce in the project.

WORKSPACE COWBOYS, INCLUDING THOSE AT iOFFICE, ARE THINKING ABOUT THE WORK ENVIRONMENT IN NEW WAYS. THEY ARE LOOKING AT WORKSPACE IN TERMS OF THE WORKFORCE, RATHER THAN JUST THE BUILDINGS AND PHYSICAL ASSETS.

The project was christened with a name that captured the identity of the firm and the notion of excellence. (The project name was so creative and company-specific that we are not mentioning it here in the interest of customer confidentiality.) Employees participated in other ways. For example, they chose the names for the conference rooms on their floors. They also developed some "soft rules" about how to behave in the new workspace (see sidebar: "Getting over the Low-Wall Hurdle").

Another success factor was the role of senior management. The Chief Global Operations Officer was engaged as the executive sponsor very early in the process. Also ready for change were the CEO (Chief Executive Officer) and CFO (Chief Financial Officer). "*Our Chairman is 100 percent behind this,*" emphasized the Project Manager. "*If you don't have that, you won't be successful.*" Trailblazing in

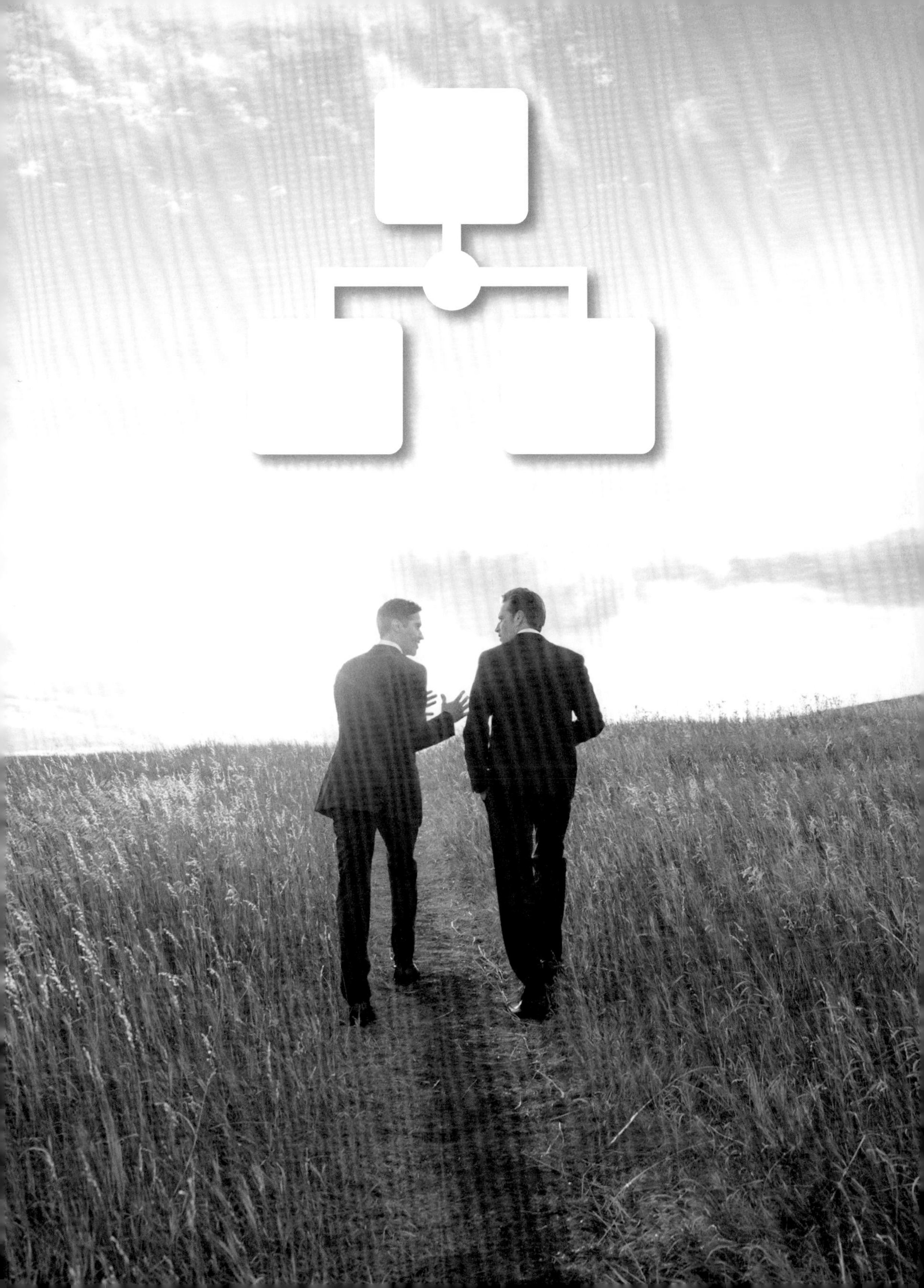

CONTEMPORARY BIZ

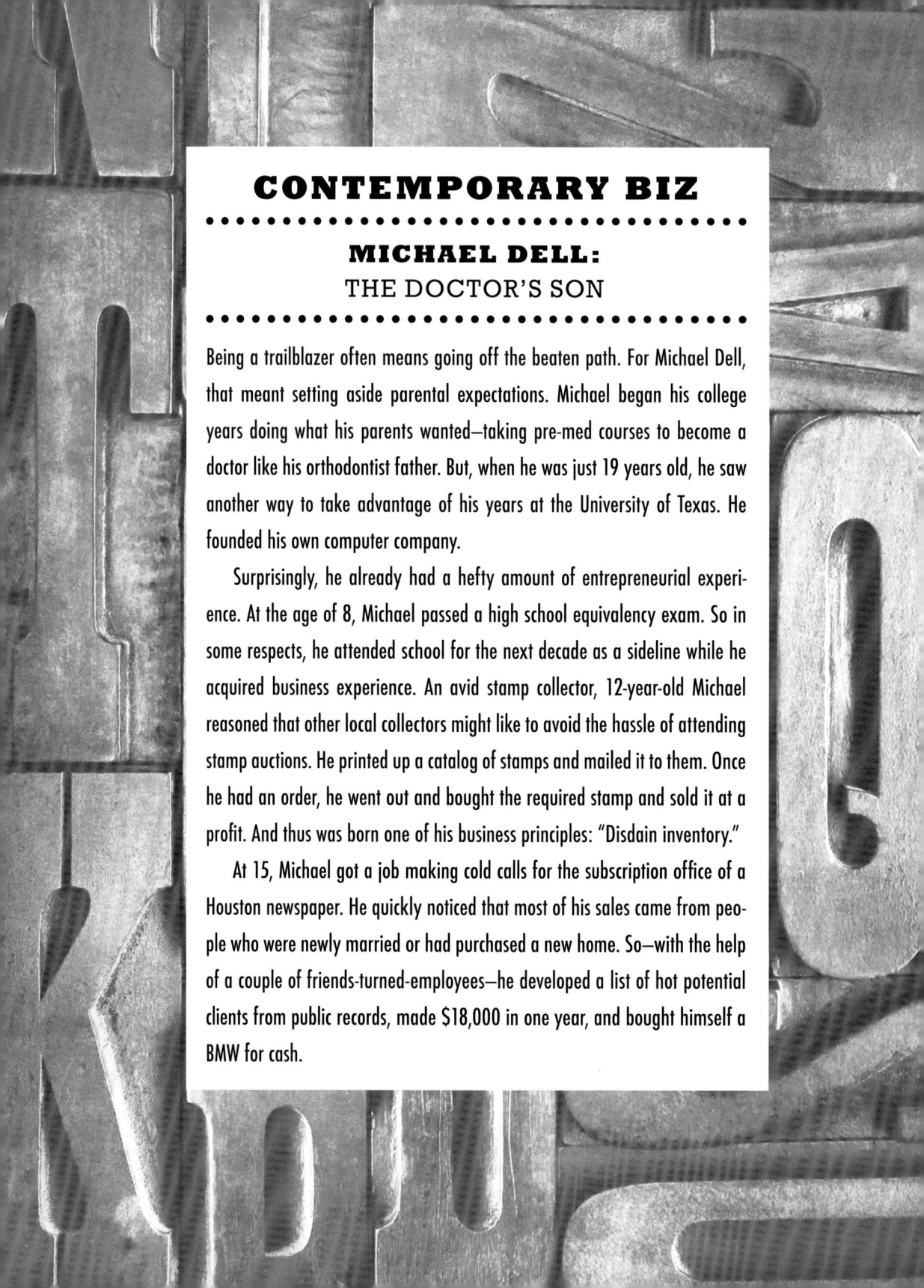

MICHAEL DELL:
THE DOCTOR'S SON

Being a trailblazer often means going off the beaten path. For Michael Dell, that meant setting aside parental expectations. Michael began his college years doing what his parents wanted—taking pre-med courses to become a doctor like his orthodontist father. But, when he was just 19 years old, he saw another way to take advantage of his years at the University of Texas. He founded his own computer company.

Surprisingly, he already had a hefty amount of entrepreneurial experience. At the age of 8, Michael passed a high school equivalency exam. So in some respects, he attended school for the next decade as a sideline while he acquired business experience. An avid stamp collector, 12-year-old Michael reasoned that other local collectors might like to avoid the hassle of attending stamp auctions. He printed up a catalog of stamps and mailed it to them. Once he had an order, he went out and bought the required stamp and sold it at a profit. And thus was born one of his business principles: "Disdain inventory."

At 15, Michael got a job making cold calls for the subscription office of a Houston newspaper. He quickly noticed that most of his sales came from people who were newly married or had purchased a new home. So—with the help of a couple of friends-turned-employees—he developed a list of hot potential clients from public records, made $18,000 in one year, and bought himself a BMW for cash.

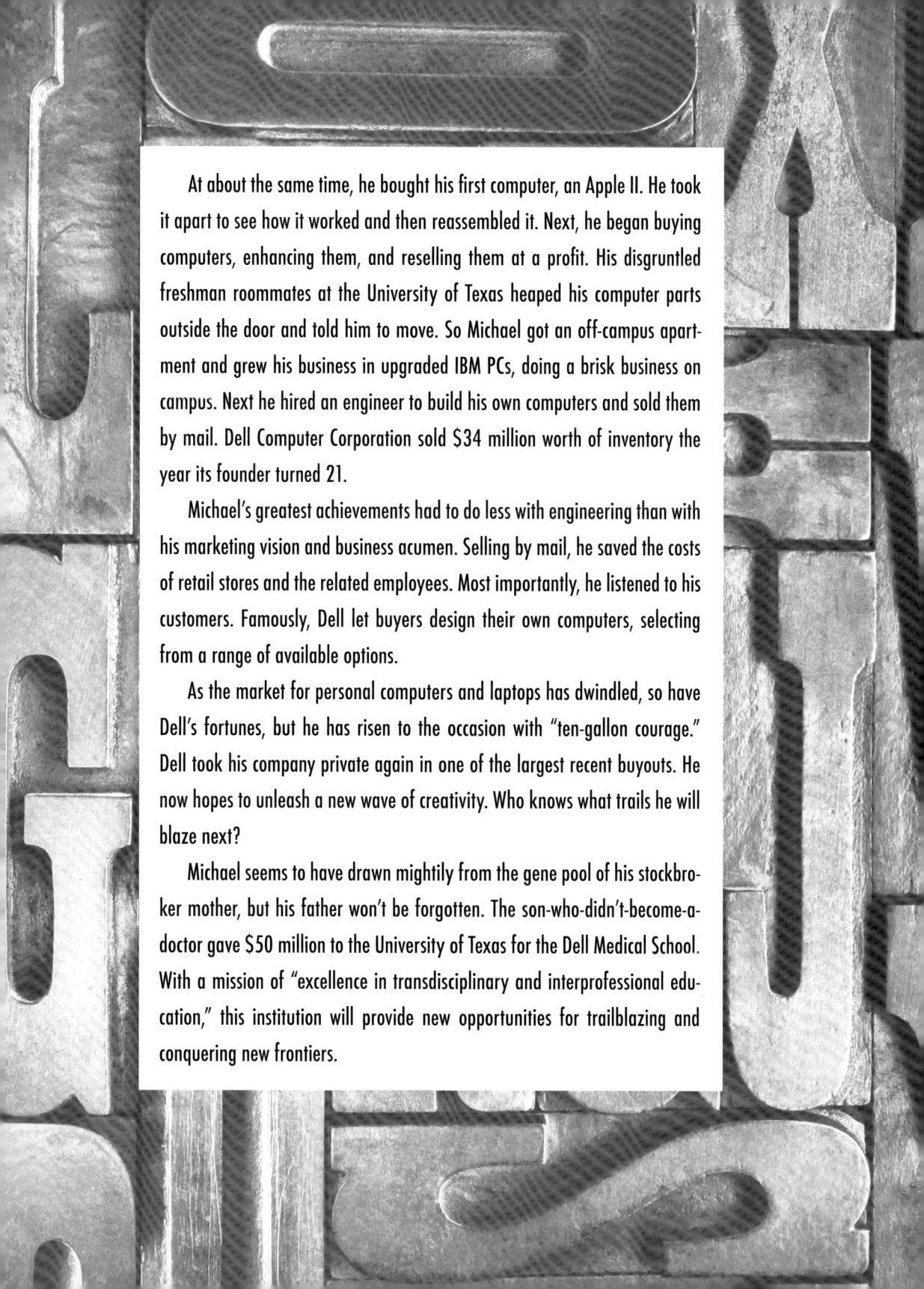

At about the same time, he bought his first computer, an Apple II. He took it apart to see how it worked and then reassembled it. Next, he began buying computers, enhancing them, and reselling them at a profit. His disgruntled freshman roommates at the University of Texas heaped his computer parts outside the door and told him to move. So Michael got an off-campus apartment and grew his business in upgraded IBM PCs, doing a brisk business on campus. Next he hired an engineer to build his own computers and sold them by mail. Dell Computer Corporation sold $34 million worth of inventory the year its founder turned 21.

Michael's greatest achievements had to do less with engineering than with his marketing vision and business acumen. Selling by mail, he saved the costs of retail stores and the related employees. Most importantly, he listened to his customers. Famously, Dell let buyers design their own computers, selecting from a range of available options.

As the market for personal computers and laptops has dwindled, so have Dell's fortunes, but he has risen to the occasion with "ten-gallon courage." Dell took his company private again in one of the largest recent buyouts. He now hopes to unleash a new wave of creativity. Who knows what trails he will blaze next?

Michael seems to have drawn mightily from the gene pool of his stockbroker mother, but his father won't be forgotten. The son-who-didn't-become-a-doctor gave $50 million to the University of Texas for the Dell Medical School. With a mission of "excellence in transdisciplinary and interprofessional education," this institution will provide new opportunities for trailblazing and conquering new frontiers.

this mature, established company was tackled with careful planning, a thoughtful process, and full engagement at all levels of the organization.

JUST LIKE THE CATTLE THAT WERE SCATTERED ON THE RANGE, THIS DATA HAD LIMITED VALUE. BUT, WHEN IT WAS PULLED TOGETHER BY A USEFUL TOOL, IT BROUGHT VALUE TO THE FACILITIES TEAM AND TO THE ENTERPRISE AS A WHOLE.

SOMETIMES BLAZING A new trail requires some new tools. That was the case with a global software company whose innovations have made it one of the top competitors in its field. The company's trailblazing mentality extends to the executives responsible for workspace management.

To serve over 20,000 customers in more than 100 countries, a large percentage of the workforce travels and/or works offsite for a majority of the time. Because the global software company makes extensive use of flexspace, the company wanted a solution to reserve space that would be easy and convenient for its employees. A survey of the market found no product that met all of their needs. So, the software firm partnered with iOffice and we have built a mobile solution that creates and tracks flexspace reservations. Unlike desktop systems, this module will give mobile workers a resource anytime, anyplace—on their smartphones.

The relationship between iOffice and the global software company also illustrates another cowboy code— Cowboys Share around the Campfire (see Code #7). The

Corporate & Facilities Services Representatives collaborated closely with iOffice to define their business requirements, responded to the new software during the development phase, and proposed refinements in the functionality. That sharing ensures that the new iOffice module will support not only employees at the software company but also the mobile workforces of other iOffice customers.

If this global enterprise is to keep blazing trails for its customers, it must optimize the output of its existing talent and incorporate more innovative, smart talent. By finding new ways to configure and manage the company's facilities, the Workspace Cowboys at this corporation are contributing to top performance in a world transformed by mobility, the cloud, and innovations as yet unknown.

BLAZING TRAILS AT iOFFICE

Through our partnerships with many of our customers, iOffice seeks to blaze new trails. Almost 15 years ago, we had a breakthrough idea that has become the core of our business model. At that time, most companies providing software services installed the programs on the client's hardware. If the software needed upgrades or repairs, the client had to do the job or wait until the provider's employees could show up.

We asked: Why not house the software in the then-developing cloud? If a problem occurs, we probably will detect and fix it before the client is aware of it. If the client discovers it first, they can call us, and we can fix it without burdening their IT department or incurring costly, time-consuming travel. Better still, our clients

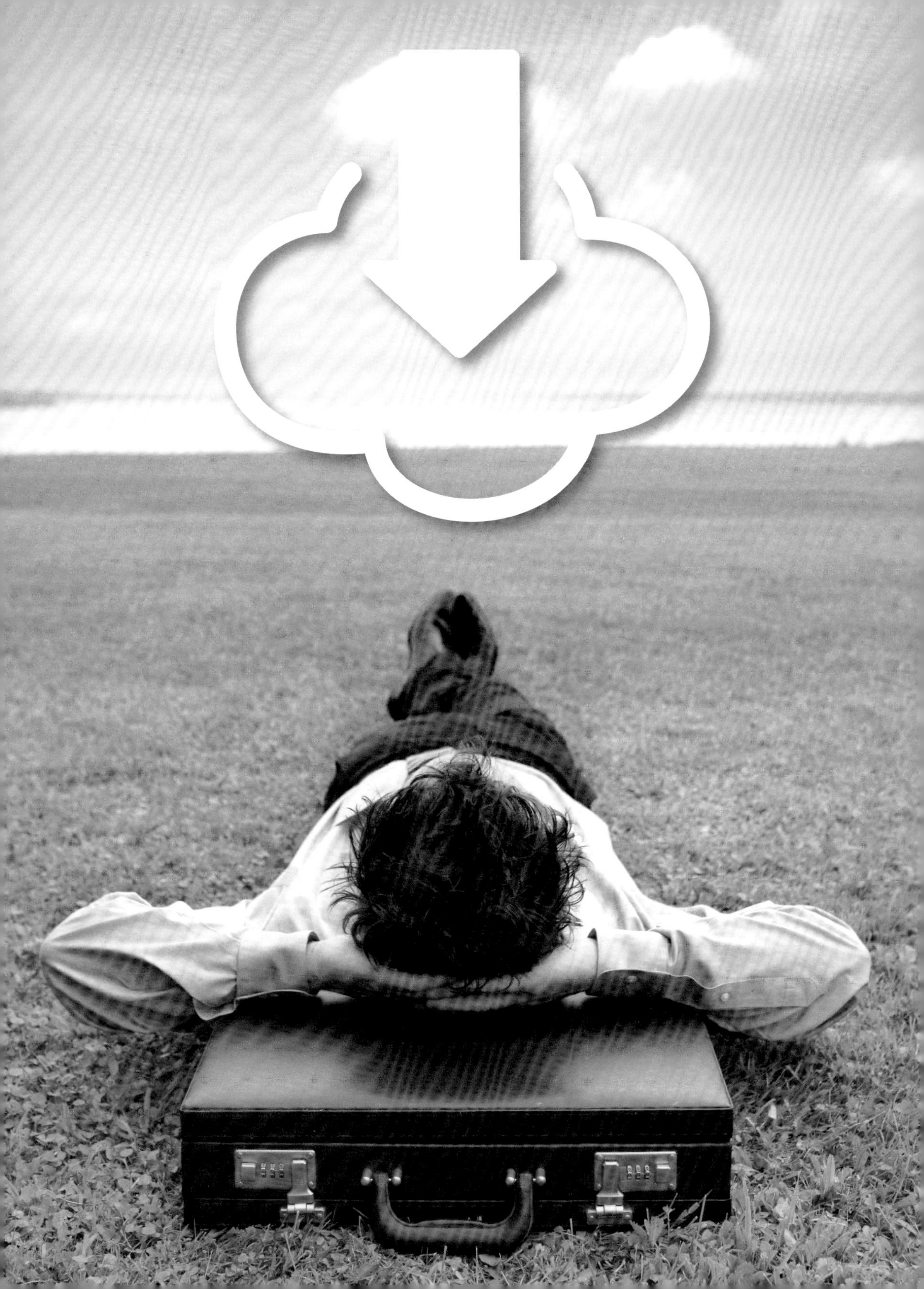

could benefit immediately from continuous upgrades to a centralized software package that would herd all of their different activities into one spot!

The iOffice platform was born. We developed a cloud-based portal to manage disparate locations in real time. The software pulled together facilities data that was previously scattered around on spreadsheets in dispersed databases and locations. Just like the cattle that were scattered on the range, this data had limited value. But, when it was pulled together by a useful tool, it brought value to the Facilities Team and to the enterprise as a whole. The ten different modules of the iOffice platform allow the user to conduct diverse activities and services through a single interface—from anywhere in the world via the Internet. When we did this, we were definitely blazing a new trail. We are proud to have been among the first to see the power of the cloud to make life easier for and add more value to our clients.

Trailblazers don't rest on their laurels. They keep looking for new territory to conquer. Workspace Cowboys, including those at iOffice, are thinking about the work environment in new ways. They are looking at workspace in terms of the workforce, rather than just the buildings and physical assets. Workspace Cowboys are inventing ways for workers to be productive in any space, at any time. At iOffice, our current trailblazing seeks to help companies manage their mobile herd, to help them deliver the right kinds of space and services to support productivity and collaboration. Working together, we will find new solutions that support the transition into the Wide Open Workspace.

VOICE OF THE CUSTOMER

GETTING OVER THE LOW-WALL HURDLE

A financial services company found that taking a new trail from high-walled cubicles to low walls raised concerns from the workforce. In fact, lowering the walls and placing the cubes in a U to encourage collaboration led to a major pushback by the workforce.

The biggest concerns were noise and privacy. So, the change agent team developed some rules of the road for the new workspace—created by employees, for employees. These "soft rules" did not come from the Project Manager or the Facilities Team or the C-suite.* "Because the employees actually wrote the rules, they are empowered to tell someone to clean off their workstation," explained the Project Manager.

For each of the six rules, the employees prepared a detailed explanation of the benefit of the new design and the behavior needed to make it work. We have shown the detail for the first rule, *Be Considerate of Your Neighbor*, which dealt specifically with the concerns of noise and privacy.

---

* *C-suite* is a term for a company's most important senior executives, whose titles tend to start with the letter "C," for "Chief," as in Chief Executive Officer, Chief Operating Officer, Chief Financial Officer, and Chief Information Officer.

BE CONSIDERATE OF YOUR NEIGHBOR

Our new workspace gives us the opportunity to collaborate and connect with each other in new and dynamic ways. To ensure that this is a productive work environment, we must make privacy and noise level concerns a top priority. While a new system has been installed to reduce noise carryover, it is critical that everyone understands the impact of noise levels on the workspace and adheres to the following guidelines:

- Keep your voice within an acceptable range to minimize disruption to others.
- Be aware of your neighbors while holding conference calls or meetings at your desk.
- Consider using a huddle room or reserving a conference room for extended conference calls, presentations, and meetings.
- Use a huddle room or conference room for private telephone and face-to-face conversations.
- Limit the use of speakerphones to conference rooms and enclosed spaces.

Similar detail was written for the following five additional rules:

- *Respect Our Workspace*
- *Maximize the Use of Team Spaces*
- *Treat Group Spaces as If You Were at Home*
- *Keep Noise Levels Down in Quiet Rooms*
- *Ensure Break Areas Remain Neat*

In post-renovation satisfaction surveys, people did not complain about the low walls. Sometimes the best way to get people to follow you down a new trail is to let them lead.

ROUNDUP

CODE #2: COWBOYS GET TOGETHER FOR THE ROUNDUP

COLLABORATION HAS BECOME a watchword in a complex and specialized world. This code explores the need to work across disciplines in order to implement projects and achieve personal and company objectives. As Workspace Cowboys work with other departments, outside vendors, and strategic partners, we are reminded of cowboys at a roundup.

Cowboys might have been lonesome, but they were rarely alone. Although each cowboy rode his own pony, the work of gathering a herd and taking it to market was a team effort. In a roundup, skilled cowboys and specially trained horses cut cattle from the herd, while others roped them, and still others held them down and branded them. A crew of at least ten cowboys was required to move the cattle along the trail. Each cowboy had more than one horse, so another member of the cattle drive team tended to the needs of the animals. Still another member of the team was responsible for the chuck wagon.

Although strong teamwork requires trust, it may also require confronting issues—dealing with problems before they can fester. In the cowboy code, if someone messed up, the crew would hold a "mock trial" at the end of the day and agree upon a punishment. They developed and enforced the rules about how they would work and live together. Similar behavior characterizes strong teams in the workplace.

COLLABORATION IN THE WORKSPACE ARENA

As service providers, Facilities Teams have always had to listen to and work with other departments to put desks and equipment in the right place or to install the AC control where the temperature can be adjusted without undue tampering. With a growing workforce and with technology as a business-enabler, Facilities Managers must work closely with HR and IT to plan for space and execute moves. Today, as companies transform their spaces and work methods, the Facilities Representative is not just one more team player. He or she leads the charge to create an environment to enhance collaboration throughout the organization.

Workspace Cowboys help project teams connect and collaborate, whether for a short-term task or for the long term. In addition, work goes wherever the employee goes. Therefore, the Facilities professionals must work with IT to manage the connections of cell phones, tablets, and other devices that tie workers together. The closer that web is woven, the more likely the company will be to succeed. The right connections allow workers to participate in the roundup, even when they are located across town or on the opposite side of the globe.

And the facilities workspace is no exception. They too must leverage technology to empower their own teamwork across diverse tasks and often across widespread locations.

Let's look at a couple of iOffice customers who demonstrate the power of collaboration, within and beyond their companies.

Our first example comes from a retailer that was growing rapidly in terms of the number of locations and associates to serve a large, diverse customer base. That growth created a large number of employee moves—a challenge that we will describe in more detail in Code #4 (Cowboys Take Pride in Their Chores). For now, we will simply mention that this retailer implemented the iOffice Space Management Module to coordinate and streamline that process.

THE FACILITIES WORKSPACE IS NO EXCEPTION. THEY TOO MUST LEVERAGE TECHNOLOGY TO EMPOWER THEIR OWN TEAMWORK ACROSS DIVERSE TASKS AND OFTEN ACROSS WIDESPREAD LOCATIONS.

After that iOffice tool was implemented, the Corporate & Facilities Services Representatives at this retailer recognized the potential to help other departments enhance their teamwork and space optimization. The iOffice platform allows the company to model different scenarios for a specific floor plan, known as "restacking." When a department wishes to optimize its space and performance, the Facilities

COWBOY HISTORY

COWBOY SKILLS:
FROM ROUNDUPS TO RODEOS

When much of Texas was untamed land, cattle roamed freely on the open range in a semi-wild state for most of the year. But every spring and fall, that freedom was interrupted by the roundup. Cowboys from several different ranches would work together, riding in great circles to gradually bring the scattered animals into a single place. There, the young calves could be branded and the mature animals sorted out for sale.

Sorting, or "cutting," specific animals from the herd required a high level of skill by cowboys riding cutting horses that were trained to move with the cattle and stop and turn faster than other horses could. Different skills were needed to rope the young calves and hold them down to be branded. Often the bulls (the male calves) were castrated. Some cattle were separated for breeding.

Rounding up the cattle was hard work for the cowboys and their horses; a cowboy might use three or four fresh horses in a single day. Therefore, the roundup tradition included a roundup of the horses that would do this work. Many young foals born to tame mares were released to grow up on the open range like wild mustangs. Mustangs and their semi-wild cousins were rounded up and tamed. Horse breaking, or "bronc busting," was usually performed by cowboys, sometimes called wranglers, who specialized in training horses.

As cowboys sought to prove their cattle- and horse-handling skills, informal competitions arose. It was not long before the necessary tasks of the working cowboy became the sport that we know today as the rodeo.

Team looks for ways to reconfigure existing space to support collaboration for that specific group. Once the best configuration is selected, the Facilities Representatives use the iOffice platform to schedule and generate the move requests needed. The results: seamless moves for departments undergoing transitions and the ability to track space, occupants, and assets on an ongoing basis. In other words, Facilities Managers can keep track of what employee is in which office and with what equipment. Likewise, they have an inventory of the conference and breakout rooms, along with their respective furniture and audiovisual support systems.

THIS RETAILER WAS ABLE TO GET TOGETHER FOR THE ROUNDUP, WITH EACH AREA BRINGING ITS SKILLSETS AND EXPERTISE TO CREATE VALUE FOR THE CORPORATION, USING THE TOOLS AVAILABLE—IN THIS CASE, THE SOFTWARE OF iOFFICE.

This retailer was able to get together for the roundup, with each area bringing its skillsets and expertise to create value for the corporation, using the tools available—in this case, the software of iOffice. As the benefits of the system became clear, the company expanded its use of the platform to support additional functions. Today, the iOffice platform is used to coordinate facility work orders, track assets, deliver mail, help control the inventory of facility supplies, manage the centralized printing center, and register visitors. All of these functionalities are "rounded up" in a single iOffice tool that takes advantage of cloud capabilities.

CONTEMPORARY BIZ

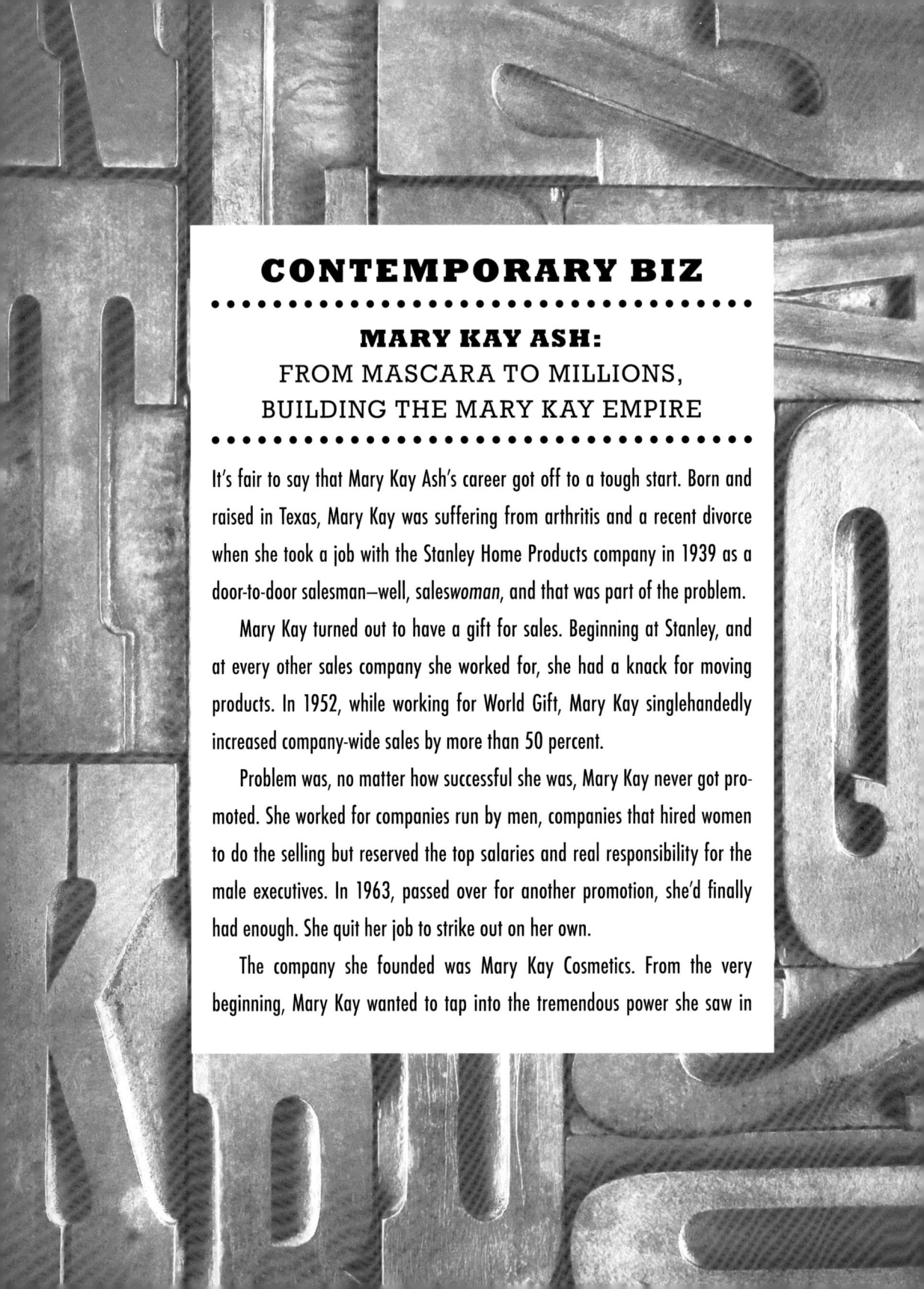

• •

MARY KAY ASH:
FROM MASCARA TO MILLIONS, BUILDING THE MARY KAY EMPIRE

• •

It's fair to say that Mary Kay Ash's career got off to a tough start. Born and raised in Texas, Mary Kay was suffering from arthritis and a recent divorce when she took a job with the Stanley Home Products company in 1939 as a door-to-door salesman—well, sales*woman*, and that was part of the problem.

Mary Kay turned out to have a gift for sales. Beginning at Stanley, and at every other sales company she worked for, she had a knack for moving products. In 1952, while working for World Gift, Mary Kay singlehandedly increased company-wide sales by more than 50 percent.

Problem was, no matter how successful she was, Mary Kay never got promoted. She worked for companies run by men, companies that hired women to do the selling but reserved the top salaries and real responsibility for the male executives. In 1963, passed over for another promotion, she'd finally had enough. She quit her job to strike out on her own.

The company she founded was Mary Kay Cosmetics. From the very beginning, Mary Kay wanted to tap into the tremendous power she saw in women like herself. In fact, her whole company structure and philosophy were designed to be supportive and collaborative. She paid her salespeople more than her competitors did, and she offered enterprising women the opportunity to build their own networks of salespeople (a technique that is still in wide use today). "Instead of a door marked *For Men Only*, our company opened its doors wide with welcome—especially for women," she remarked.

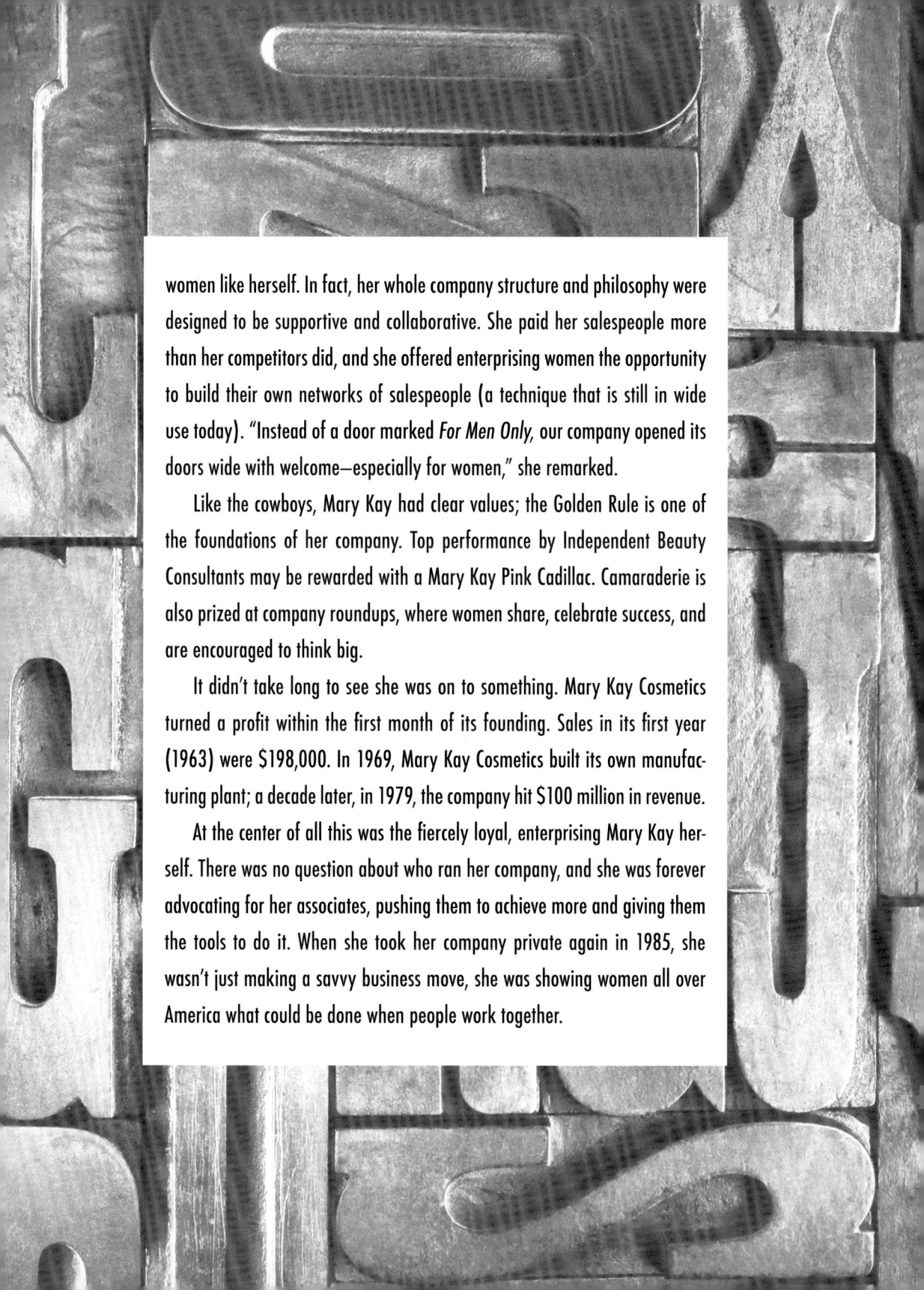

Like the cowboys, Mary Kay had clear values; the Golden Rule is one of the foundations of her company. Top performance by Independent Beauty Consultants may be rewarded with a Mary Kay Pink Cadillac. Camaraderie is also prized at company roundups, where women share, celebrate success, and are encouraged to think big.

It didn't take long to see she was on to something. Mary Kay Cosmetics turned a profit within the first month of its founding. Sales in its first year (1963) were $198,000. In 1969, Mary Kay Cosmetics built its own manufacturing plant; a decade later, in 1979, the company hit $100 million in revenue.

At the center of all this was the fiercely loyal, enterprising Mary Kay herself. There was no question about who ran her company, and she was forever advocating for her associates, pushing them to achieve more and giving them the tools to do it. When she took her company private again in 1985, she wasn't just making a savvy business move, she was showing women all over America what could be done when people work together.

WIDE OPEN WORKSPACE

At the roundup, skilled cowboys worked as a team to leverage their assets (such as specially trained horses) and diverse skills (such as roping and branding). When a new management team joined this major retailer a few years ago, there was a roundup of diverse talents (different functions and vendors) to familiarize the new managers with the power of the iOffice portal and the tools embedded therein. By understanding expectations, providing training, and illustrating the benefits of the system, these Workspace Cowboys helped to ensure that the company would continue reaping the benefits of its investment in space management technology. Today, this retailer uses all the modules of the iOffice portal to achieve performance not only in space management but as a partner to the office and facility services business as a whole.

WHEN WORKSPACE COWBOYS PULL THEIR SKILLS TOGETHER, THEY ARE ABLE TO ADD VALUE TO THE HERD, CREATING THE ENVIRONMENTS THAT SUPPORT COLLABORATION, AN ESSENTIAL INGREDIENT FOR TODAY'S BUSINESS SUCCESS.

ONE OF OUR customers in the global energy business recently built a new LEED Platinum office building for its Texas headquarters. The building is designed to promote sustainability and create an engaging office environment to attract and keep talented employees. As the building reached completion, the Corporate & Facilities Services Representative faced the daunting task of relocating

VOICE OF THE CUSTOMER

COLLABORATION TO ACHIEVE COLLABORATION

The Corporate & Facilities Services Representative at a global energy company shared how he partners with other departments to help enhance teamwork.

"In this company, there is a lot of emphasis on collaboration, so we designed the building to maximize it. We have conference rooms and collaboration rooms all over the building. They're always booked. People like to get out of their office and get into meetings and work together. The new configuration has been very well received.

"Our growth, the changing dynamics of the core business, and the changing workforce has forced us to deliver space and facilities differently, especially to the people who are on the move and in the field. It's challenging, because the business is very fluid. Depending on where we're focusing, people will be relocated within the business to enhance their working together. In two years, they might be somewhere different.

"The Facilities Team plays an important role in what we can achieve as a company. As the business has evolved and grown, we have a seat at the table. Instead of somebody else deciding what we're going to do and telling us to go do it, we are part of the conversation from the beginning. Now we might hear, 'Tell us what you think, based on your knowledge and expertise about the building and how people work.' Senior management gives us a chance to sit with them and communicate. They don't always go with our ideas, but they hear us out.

"To be seen as a problem solver, it really gets down to understanding the space and how it can be used. A department head might come to me and say, 'Hey, I've got 20 people coming. I only have five spots left on my floor. What do I do?' They come and ask for help.

"I offer them different solutions. For example, I might say, 'Look, I can turn this room into a hot-desk area where your people can move in and out.' Or I might suggest 'hoteling,' by which you book people to use the space when they are here at headquarters. I might say, 'What do you think about installing eight desks that can be shared and 20 rolling file cabinets?' The department heads didn't know they could do that. Working together, we figure out the best way to utilize the space."

CONTEMPORARY BIZ

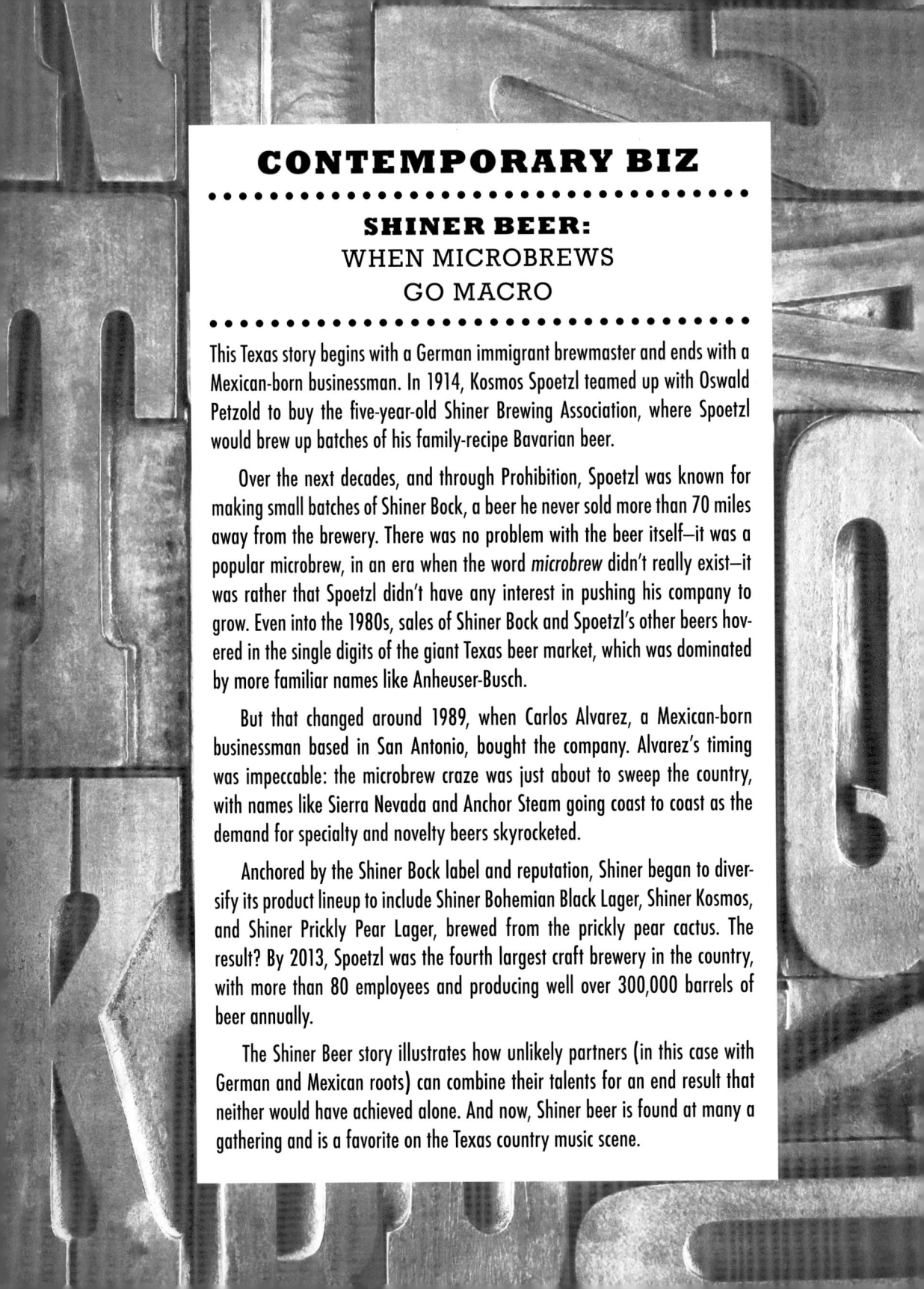

SHINER BEER:
WHEN MICROBREWS GO MACRO

This Texas story begins with a German immigrant brewmaster and ends with a Mexican-born businessman. In 1914, Kosmos Spoetzl teamed up with Oswald Petzold to buy the five-year-old Shiner Brewing Association, where Spoetzl would brew up batches of his family-recipe Bavarian beer.

Over the next decades, and through Prohibition, Spoetzl was known for making small batches of Shiner Bock, a beer he never sold more than 70 miles away from the brewery. There was no problem with the beer itself—it was a popular microbrew, in an era when the word *microbrew* didn't really exist—it was rather that Spoetzl didn't have any interest in pushing his company to grow. Even into the 1980s, sales of Shiner Bock and Spoetzl's other beers hovered in the single digits of the giant Texas beer market, which was dominated by more familiar names like Anheuser-Busch.

But that changed around 1989, when Carlos Alvarez, a Mexican-born businessman based in San Antonio, bought the company. Alvarez's timing was impeccable: the microbrew craze was just about to sweep the country, with names like Sierra Nevada and Anchor Steam going coast to coast as the demand for specialty and novelty beers skyrocketed.

Anchored by the Shiner Bock label and reputation, Shiner began to diversify its product lineup to include Shiner Bohemian Black Lager, Shiner Kosmos, and Shiner Prickly Pear Lager, brewed from the prickly pear cactus. The result? By 2013, Spoetzl was the fourth largest craft brewery in the country, with more than 80 employees and producing well over 300,000 barrels of beer annually.

The Shiner Beer story illustrates how unlikely partners (in this case with German and Mexican roots) can combine their talents for an end result that neither would have achieved alone. And now, Shiner beer is found at many a gathering and is a favorite on the Texas country music scene.

1,800 employees and minimizing the impact of that move on their productivity. This corporation already had the iOffice tool, allowing the management team to plan the entire move from the old building to the new.

BY BRINGING A LEVEL OF SOPHISTICATION TO THE FACILITIES TEAM, THE SOFTWARE EMPOWERED THEM TO ENGAGE MANAGEMENT, EMPLOYEES, AND SUPPORTING VENDORS IN THE MOVE.

Current office floor plans and employee locations were already in the system. The next step was to upload the new building's floor plans. The Facilities Representative was then able to create scenarios for moving employees and assets. Executives could see and approve the floor plans for their departments. The on-line plans allowed immediate adjustments throughout the occupancy design process; the Facilities Team could adapt on the fly and coordinate the moves in a real-time, shared schedule. The software created tactical details that defined where, when, and how everyone would relocate to the new space. By bringing a level of sophistication to the Facilities Team, the software empowered them to engage management, employees, and supporting vendors in the move.

In the new location, some services are provided by the global energy company and some by the real estate company that manages the new building. Both parties worked together with iOffice to create a single, seamless solution for all the workers in the building. When a service issue arises, the employee submits one on-line service request

COWBOY HISTORY

THE UNIVERSITY OF TEXAS SYSTEM:
COLLEGIATE COLLABORATION FOR FIRST-CLASS RESULTS

In 1883, a professor of chemistry named Dr. John W. Mallet stood on a hill in Austin before a crowd of hopeful Texans and spoke these words: "If Texas is to have a university of the first class . . . its development must be the result of the united efforts of the people of Texas, of the state government, of the Board of Regents, of the faculty, and above all, of the students of the university."

With those words, he consecrated the University of Texas at Austin, the flagship of the UT System, which has become one of the great universities in America. Since then, the UT System has raked in academic honors and collected armloads of national sports titles, without ever losing its unique place in Texas lore.

Springing as it does from the fertile intellectual ground of Austin, UT underscores one of the little-appreciated traits that has made Texas great. Although the name the *Lone Star State* conjures up an image of the rugged individual, the lone cowboy swinging down the trail, Texas was, in fact, built by millions of people working closely together. Just about everything that makes Texas great—from the gleaming corporate skyscrapers in Dallas to the championship Dallas Cowboys—is the product of many people, men and women, all pulling together and working hard for the same goal.

In that fall of 1883, Dr. Mallet set the expectation that the roundup mentality would guide the state's university to first-class results. What do those results look like today?

- *Nine universities that educate more than 200,000 students and award more than 45,000 degrees annually*

- *Six healthcare institutions that provide over one million days of hospital treatment and serve six million outpatients each year*

- *A spirit of innovation, reflected in $2.5 billion of research funding and millions of dollars of technology commercialization*

That mindset is still clear in the vision of the current chancellor, Francisco G. Cigarroa, who is a champion of collaboration and creativity. Under his leadership, we can expect a university system that is guided by classical wisdom yet able to seize the moment and transcend the issues of our time.

and the tool dispatches the ticket to the appropriate party. Building on an existing solution meant streamlined service for the end user.

THIS MAN WAS A NEWCOMER, ENTERING AN ESTABLISHED COMPANY THAT HAD BEEN MANAGING AND DELIVERING FACILITY SERVICES THE OLD-FASHIONED WAY. AS A WORKSPACE COWBOY, HE WAS BOLD ENOUGH TO SAY, "THIS WILL NOT WORK. I CANNOT EFFECTIVELY DELIVER SERVICES TO MY CUSTOMERS."

iOFFICE AND THE ROUNDUP

We rely on teamwork for the future development and enhancement of our own product—teamwork within our own professional staff, teamwork with our customers, and sometimes teamwork with other players in the software space.

The code Cowboys Get Together for the Roundup inspires us to be team players. Each person has a specific task and plays an important part in getting a job done. We work as a team, not just as a company but also with our customers. When Workspace Cowboys pull their skills together, they are able to add value to the herd, creating the environments that support collaboration, an essential ingredient for today's business success.

COURAGE

CODE #3: COWBOYS HAVE TEN-GALLON COURAGE TO DO WHAT NEEDS TO BE DONE

FACILITIES MANAGERS work hard to keep things running smoothly, but problems and challenges will arise. Even if your company is not in the midst of a major change, there is plenty that can go wrong. This code is about having the courage to do what it takes to get the job done, whether you are managing the physical assets of the company or trying to embrace the changing workforce dynamics. What can we learn from the cowboys about finding our way through some pretty unfriendly territory?

Texas was an uninviting space for those who came to settle there in the early 1800s. Like any frontier, it tended to attract people who weren't leaving much behind; some were actually on the run from their past. It was a dry and dusty place, and intensely hot for part of the year.

It took a certain amount of fortitude to put down roots in such a place. It took a ten-gallon hat full of courage to drive a herd of cattle across it, with no map but the stars and only a vague notion of where your destination lay. Cowboys didn't make much fuss about that danger. No shivering in their boots, so to speak. They just set out together to get the job done, and a hard job it was.

Texas Longhorn cattle had been on their own for too many years to bend naturally to the will of the men who drove them. Cowboys took advantage of the cows' natural herding instincts to keep them together. That worked well, as long as you let them move along at a leisurely, grass-munching pace. If something scared them, though, that herding instinct quickly became a threat. A quietly grazing herd could turn into an angry stampede with one crash of thunder or one rattlesnake near the edge of the herd.

Although dustups with Indians and rustlers weren't as common as Hollywood suggests, they certainly presented a real danger. So did farmers on the road north, who took unkindly to a herd of cattle trampling through their fields. To be a successful cowboy, you had to be willing to take risks and believe that the destination would be worth all the trouble it took to reach it.

COURAGE IN THE WORKSPACE ARENA

Courage is not the exclusive domain of cowboys; let's watch one Facilities Manager in action. Her company purchased several buildings that they intended to use as manufacturing space. The property was a "good deal," so the company bought it and turned the buildings over to their Facilities Manager to convert them into the type of space they needed. When the Head of Manufacturing described the equipment he wanted to bring in, the Facilities Manager discovered that

COWBOY HISTORY

SAM HOUSTON:
LEGENDARY LEADER OF A NEW REPUBLIC

If Sam Houston had gone to high school—instead of spending his adolescent years hanging out with the Cherokee who lived across the Tennessee River from his family's home near Maryville—chances are no one would have voted him "most likely to become president." Instead of helping his brothers with the family farm and store, Houston adopted the Cherokee as a surrogate family and took their chief, Oolooteka, as a surrogate for his own father, who died when Sam was 13.

Although Houston had little education himself, at age 18 he set up a school as a way to earn money. He served with General Andrew Jackson in the War of 1812, getting the attention of the man who was on his way to the White House. With this political connection, Houston quickly rose to become a congressman for Tennessee and then governor of that state.

For the most part, Houston remained out of the spotlight until December 2, 1832, when, as he was about to turn 40, he crossed the Red River into Texas and walked into the pages of history. Gossip is rampant over exactly why he made this crucial decision: Was he just one of the many land speculators drawn to the Texas territory by the absence of governmental authority? Was he a secret agent working toward making that region part of the United States? Or had he seen a vision of himself as the founding father of a new Republic of Texas?

Whatever the truth, Sam Houston was a man with the charisma and the connections that suited the times. He promptly put himself in the middle of the movement to win Texas's independence from Mexico. Mexico itself was newly independent from Spain and in considerable political turmoil. Although Houston established a law practice, he began to speak loudly on behalf of war and soon was named commander in chief of the local armed forces. After negotiating a treaty with the local Cherokee, his birthday gift in 1836 was the Texas Declaration of Independence, signed at a convention of Texas leaders.

Houston was named major general of the Texas Army. After an initial retreat from a skirmish with the Mexican Army at Gonzales, Houston led his small corps to defeat the much larger forces of General Antonio López de Santa Anna, capturing the Mexican leader. Much to the surprise of many who had known him before his crossing into Texas, Sam Houston had now become the stuff of legend.

Houston was the first elected president of the Republic of Texas. He negotiated treaties with the Indian tribes remaining in Texas and skirted military confrontations with Mexico. He carried the flag for annexation with the United States, served two terms as senator, and was governor at the advent of the Civil War. Foreseeing the devastation the war would bring, Houston refused to sign an oath of loyalty to the Confederate States of America and was removed from office. Although he died in the shadows of war, the legend of Sam Houston survived to make him the widely acknowledged Father of Texas.

the buildings were built on concrete slabs that were only four inches thick. They could not support the equipment!

Needless to say, this was unwelcome news. Management said, "You've gotta make this happen. We can't shut down." With her back against the wall, the Facilities Manager had to search for a solution and insist on investing in some reforms that were essential to the long-term safety of the equipment and its operators.

In talking about her situation, she said, *"I know that if things go badly, I'm gonna hear about it. But if things go well, I won't hear a thing."* In addition to taking the risk to solve the problem, she must have the resolve and fortitude to possibly take the blame if things don't work out well. And, although on the front line, making things work, Facilities Managers may get no praise for all they accomplish. Being an unsung hero comes with the territory of the Workspace Cowboy.

LET'S LOOK AT another example that comes from a leading industrial gas company operating in 80 countries. About two years ago, this company hired a new Director of Corporate Facilities Services at its U.S. headquarters. He inherited a process by which maintenance requests were being received via telephone, email, and personal interaction, with limited recordkeeping. He recognized the need for a standardized process to receive requests, to track services, and to measure costs and customer satisfaction. In addition, he wanted to know which and how many team members were necessary to complete a requested service from start to finish. Benchmarks were needed to proactively forecast future resource requirements to manage facilities.

Although on the FRONT LINE, making things work, facilities managers may get no praise for all they accomplish. Being an unsung hero comes with the territory of the WORKSPACE COWBOY.

iOffice was asked by the new Director to install its cloud-based software with a robust menu of service requests that were customized to his company. He chose iOffice because its system is easy for requesters to use. With one click on the company intranet, employees can access the portal, submit requests, and receive status updates and service resolutions.

The system was a boon for the Facilities Team. Some of the important functions were

- a centralized queue for receiving service requests from all facilities;
- a display of requests by type, request location, requester, submission time, assigned technician(s), and current status of each request;
- the ability for each facility to dispatch service requests to on-site staff and offsite vendors;
- the documentation of wait, start, and stop times of each request;
- customized schedules for monthly, quarterly, and annual maintenance tasks, generated automatically;
- local, regional, and corporate views of each facility's service activity in real time;

CONTEMPORARY BIZ

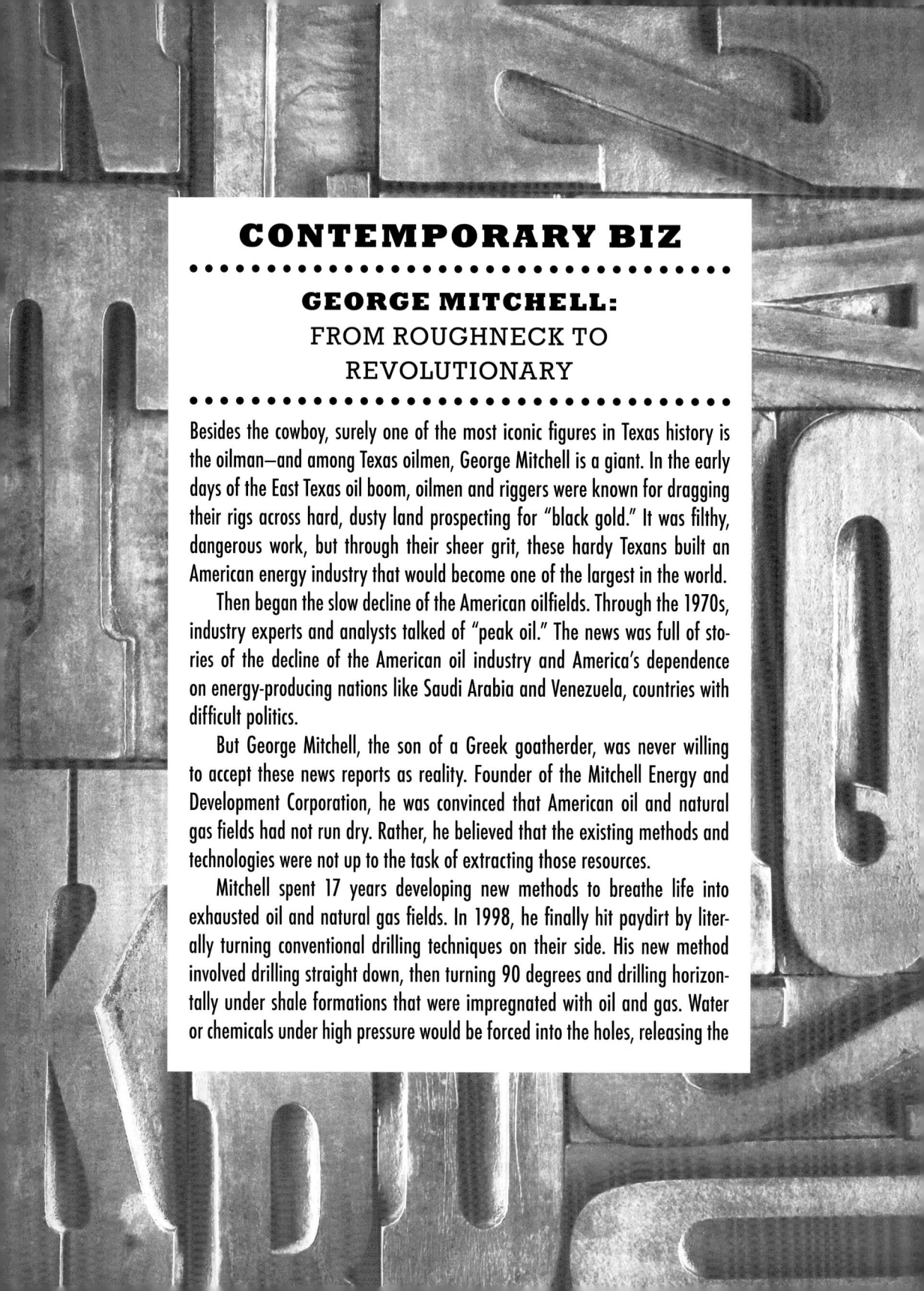

GEORGE MITCHELL:
FROM ROUGHNECK TO REVOLUTIONARY

Besides the cowboy, surely one of the most iconic figures in Texas history is the oilman—and among Texas oilmen, George Mitchell is a giant. In the early days of the East Texas oil boom, oilmen and riggers were known for dragging their rigs across hard, dusty land prospecting for "black gold." It was filthy, dangerous work, but through their sheer grit, these hardy Texans built an American energy industry that would become one of the largest in the world.

Then began the slow decline of the American oilfields. Through the 1970s, industry experts and analysts talked of "peak oil." The news was full of stories of the decline of the American oil industry and America's dependence on energy-producing nations like Saudi Arabia and Venezuela, countries with difficult politics.

But George Mitchell, the son of a Greek goatherder, was never willing to accept these news reports as reality. Founder of the Mitchell Energy and Development Corporation, he was convinced that American oil and natural gas fields had not run dry. Rather, he believed that the existing methods and technologies were not up to the task of extracting those resources.

Mitchell spent 17 years developing new methods to breathe life into exhausted oil and natural gas fields. In 1998, he finally hit paydirt by literally turning conventional drilling techniques on their side. His new method involved drilling straight down, then turning 90 degrees and drilling horizontally under shale formations that were impregnated with oil and gas. Water or chemicals under high pressure would be forced into the holes, releasing the available stores of hydrocarbons. According to one estimate, this method, now known as *fracking* (short for *fracturing*), increased the productivity of oil and gas wells tenfold.

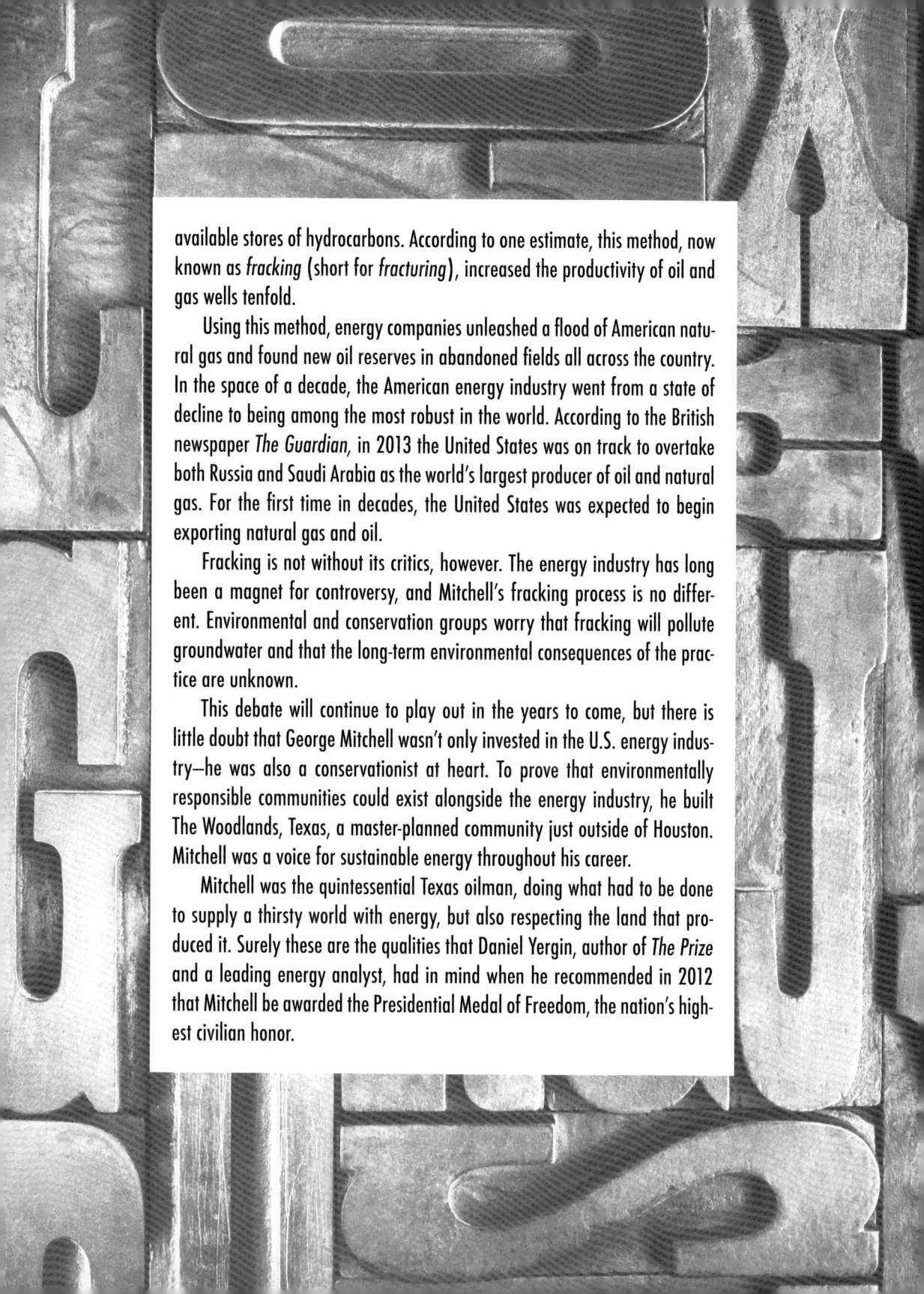

Using this method, energy companies unleashed a flood of American natural gas and found new oil reserves in abandoned fields all across the country. In the space of a decade, the American energy industry went from a state of decline to being among the most robust in the world. According to the British newspaper *The Guardian*, in 2013 the United States was on track to overtake both Russia and Saudi Arabia as the world's largest producer of oil and natural gas. For the first time in decades, the United States was expected to begin exporting natural gas and oil.

Fracking is not without its critics, however. The energy industry has long been a magnet for controversy, and Mitchell's fracking process is no different. Environmental and conservation groups worry that fracking will pollute groundwater and that the long-term environmental consequences of the practice are unknown.

This debate will continue to play out in the years to come, but there is little doubt that George Mitchell wasn't only invested in the U.S. energy industry—he was also a conservationist at heart. To prove that environmentally responsible communities could exist alongside the energy industry, he built The Woodlands, Texas, a master-planned community just outside of Houston. Mitchell was a voice for sustainable energy throughout his career.

Mitchell was the quintessential Texas oilman, doing what had to be done to supply a thirsty world with energy, but also respecting the land that produced it. Surely these are the qualities that Daniel Yergin, author of *The Prize* and a leading energy analyst, had in mind when he recommended in 2012 that Mitchell be awarded the Presidential Medal of Freedom, the nation's highest civilian honor.

VOICE OF THE CUSTOMER

METRICS TO BOLSTER YOUR COURAGE

Pushing your company to do what needs to be done takes courage or, as one iOffice customer put it, "intestinal fortitude." Where can a Workspace Cowboy find an ally when he stands up for his herd? Despite the difficulty of quantifying the benefits, help can be found in metrics, surveys, and external benchmarks.

EXTERNAL STANDARDS. "Our CFO raised a question about the amount of collaboration space we had planned and whether we needed it. Some senior managers don't tend to work as collaboratively as the workforce does, so it's hard for them to understand that someone would literally turn around in their workstation and go to a little table in the middle and meet one of their teammates to talk about something, because that's not how they work. Our architects pulled together some industry standards in terms of seats, percentage of seats per total or square foot per collaboration seat—those types of metrics—and showed that we were in line with where forward-looking companies are going."

ELUSIVE RETURN ON INVESTMENT (ROI). "When you spend a lot of money on an initiative like this, it's very difficult to measure ROI. You know intuitively, as an example, that productivity should increase, employee engagement should increase, those types of things, but it's really difficult to measure productivity in a service sector company. And most C-suite people focus on those types of metrics. We had a chairman who was willing to look beyond that. He really wanted to do something specifically for the employees. And it's very rare that you find that."

VALIDATION THROUGH THE VOICE OF THE WORKER. "We did a pre- and post-occupancy survey. The employees rated 14 different factors on a scale from one to five in terms of the importance and their level of satisfaction. The factors were things like storage space, access to conference and meeting rooms, daylight and views, ergonomic tools, and whether the workspace was comfortable. After the reconfiguration, the scores went up. Keep in mind, it's on a scale of one to five; our scores went up from less than two and a half to over four in terms of overall level of satisfaction."

Benchmarking tools by site and technician now meet the Director's reporting goals and requirements. This man was a newcomer, entering an established company that had been managing and delivering facility services the old-fashioned way. As a Workspace Cowboy, he was bold enough to say, "This will not work. I cannot effectively deliver services to my customers." He did what needed to be done to deliver higher service levels to the employees at this global enterprise, contributing to the overall results of the company.

THE iOFFICE PLATFORM AND COURAGE

Sometimes the hardest thing for facility professionals to do is to convince upper management that they *need a tool* . . . because they typically do a great job without it! Senior management just sees an additional cost, and the Facilities Team is caught in a Catch-22. Without the tool and the data it could provide, a Facilities Manager is unable to quantify the hidden and soft costs being incurred. It is hard to demonstrate the lost time and indirect costs that result from the failure to respond to the requirements of the workforce in a timely fashion.

That is the scenario in a traditional office setting. Today, however, senior management is adding a new mandate: "You need to make this workspace an attractive, flexible environment, because half of our workforce is going to go mobile and work virtually." Suddenly, you have to keep track of who's coming in and going out. You need to be sure that if a worker needs a space, one is available. Expectations are moving from basic and mundane to sophisticated requests that help attract workers and make them productive. This creates an even greater need for tools to communicate, measure, and track.

Enlightened senior managers may agree that there's a need for software to support the change, but the recommendation of a vendor rests largely with the Facilities Director. What if they make a bad decision? What if they make the wrong technology choice? What if their costs increase or system glitches make them lose credibility? If things go wrong, the Facilities Director will bear the full blame.

EXPECTATIONS ARE MOVING FROM BASIC AND MUNDANE TO SOPHISTICATED REQUESTS THAT HELP ATTRACT WORKERS AND MAKE THEM PRODUCTIVE. THIS CREATES AN EVEN GREATER NEED FOR TOOLS TO COMMUNICATE, MEASURE, AND TRACK.

In the hot seat, our unsung hero needs to find the courage to embrace change. iOffice helps by removing some of the risks of bringing in new technology. The iOffice platform is easy to use, flexible, and versatile. It provides data to support decision-making and ongoing tracking. The Workspace Cowboy can be courageous and embrace the change, without the big risk of a product that may not work or a product that is too complicated, is too expensive, or doesn't integrate into their current reality. The iOffice platform supports both the traditional office environment and the workspace of the future. Knowing he or she has a reliable, straightforward tool, the Workspace Cowboy can be prepared for whatever is coming his or her way.

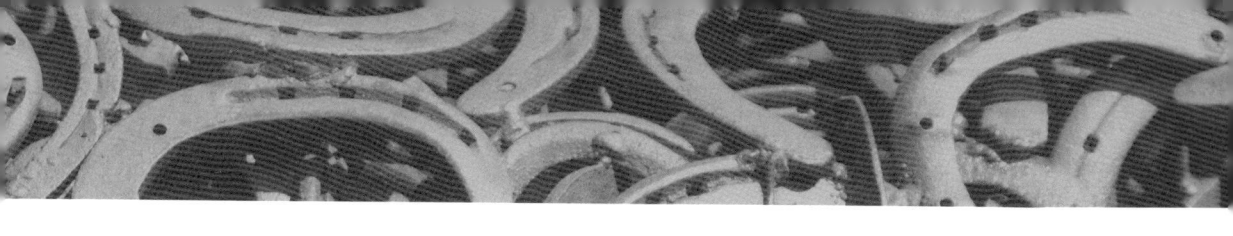

COWBOY HISTORY

HENRIETTA CHAMBERLAIN KING:
THE LADY WHO OWNED THE LARGEST RANCH IN THE WORLD

The life of Henrietta Chamberlain King may help explain why the term *cowgirl* never caught on. While there were certainly women on hand during the West's cowboy era, there was nothing girlish about them. The daughter of a Presbyterian minister, Henrietta was raised to be a lady, and though she insisted on an environment of civility that was not always common in that time and place, she was no "girly-girl."

Henrietta was introduced to her husband, Richard King, when his steamboat rammed the houseboat where she and her father then lived, and she chastised him for his foul language. King had already started to amass a land empire, but the first home he provided for Henrietta was a tiny adobe *jacal*, in the middle of the dangerous and disputed territory of the Wild Horse Prairie. Henrietta was baking bread one day when she turned around in her kitchen to find an Indian with his tomahawk raised over her infant. She handed him a loaf of bread. He decided to accept the offering and move on.

During the Civil War, Henrietta was at home alone and pregnant when Union forces came looking for her husband; Richard was smuggling Confederate cotton across the border into Mexico. After watching the soldiers ransack and plunder her home, she packed up her family and took them to safety in San Antonio.

Following the war, the King ranch grew in size, but so did Richard's debt. When he died in 1885, the red ink totaled $500,000, an enormous sum in that era. Together with Richard's legal adviser, Robert Justus Kleberg, whom she hired as the ranch manager, Henrietta wiped out the debt in the next ten years—and grew the ranch at the same time. Turning more of the ranch responsibility over to Kleberg, Henrietta invested in the infrastructure for the St. Louis, Brownsville & Mexico Railway. She put her money into land that would become the right-of-ways for the tracks and town sites for railroad employees. She also invested in services to meet the needs of those who worked on the railroad.

Before Henrietta died, the King ranch was the largest in the world. By doing what had to be done, she built her fortune with a mix of courage and compassion. From beginning to end, Henrietta had taken care of the education and health of the ranch workers, most of whom were Mexican. She always spoke Spanish on the range. Two hundred of those hands—called *kineños*, or King's men—rode with the coffin at her funeral.

VOICE OF THE CUSTOMER

COURAGE TO LOOK BEYOND THE WALLS

Sometimes decisions about workspace require Facilities Managers to raise issues and concerns that fall outside of their buildings' walls. Below, we share thoughts from two different clients about how transportation, getting to work, was a factor in planning for flexspace and for a move to a new location.

IMPLEMENTING FLEXSPACE. "When implementing flexspace, another challenge is parking. If the density of the work area increases, with no adjustment in available parking, employees must spend valuable time fighting for a place to park. The positive benefits of flexspace can quickly be eroded. This is especially challenging in areas of the country where mass transit does not exist or is not a preferred method of commuting. The situation can be even worse when employees have to face the elements when walking long distances from public lots to the office."

SEEKING A NEW LOCATION. "Looking at new office space in the central business district of a major city, we recognized that transportation was an issue. We explored how to get our employees to use mass transit. We made a deliberate choice not to locate further out, where everybody would have to drive in by car. Instead, we looked at how to get more cars off the road, with a location that would allow our employees to take mass transit. It is our job to be sensitive to that."

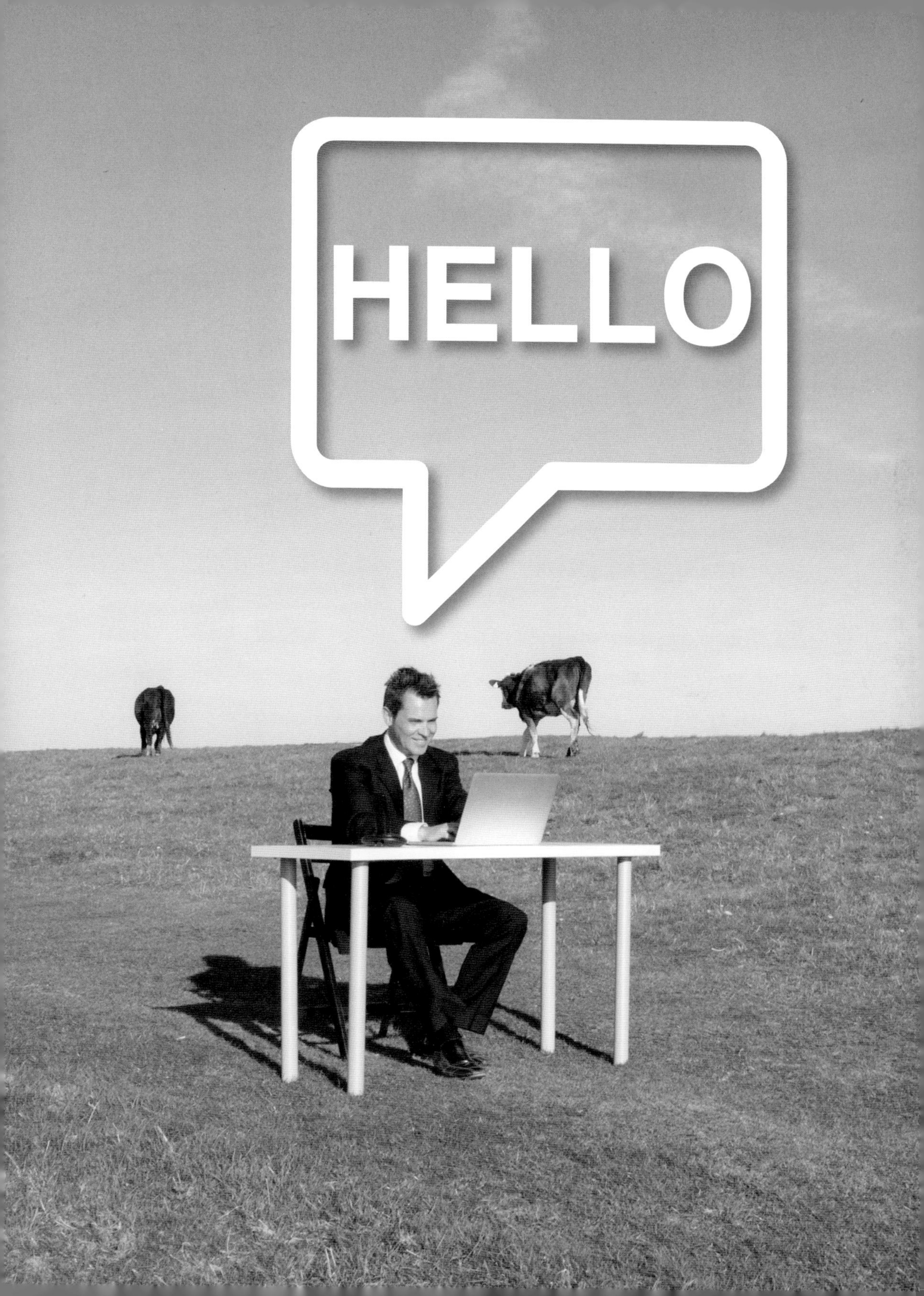
HELLO

PRIDE

CODE #4: COWBOYS TAKE PRIDE IN THEIR CHORES

COWBOYS GET PRETTY dusty. So it is for the Facilities Team members, who may recognize themselves in the following bit of Texas history.

Most cowboys didn't have a lot of formal schooling. The riding and roping skills that would later be the stuff of showy rodeos were learned down and dirty on the ranch and the trails to market. You had to be a good rider just to stay in the saddle among a herd of occasionally irascible cattle, particularly if weather or some local critters spooked them. Cowboys were assigned positions around the herd. The fellas up front had to keep a lookout for good trails and potential troublemakers. (The movie stars usually play these roles.) Just as important, though, were the guys in back who made sure no strays wandered off. Those guys ate a lot of dust in the process.

Many cowboy chores were less than glamorous. Did John Wayne ever play the cook in the chuck wagon? Probably not, and yet real cowboys depended on good nourishment to get on with the drive. Another important but far from legendary character was the hand who took care of the horses—feeding them, changing shoes, and providing medical care when needed.

A lot of the traits that made good cowboys also turned up when oil replaced cattle as a source of wealth in Texas. Just about all of the jobs in the early oilfields were dirty, and many of them were dangerous as well. Derrickhands, for example, maintained the mud pumps and pits that circulated fluids to keep the whole process free of debris during drilling. While the driller gave the orders, it was the derrickhand up on the rig itself who manipulated the machine. When a gusher came in—or, worse yet, if gas triggered an explosion—the derrickhand was on the spot.

CHORES IN WORKPLACE MANAGEMENT

Like the cowboy or the derrickhand, the Facilities Manager has to do some pretty mundane chores. Historically, managers have used the telephone, email, and spreadsheets to handle all the details behind the scenes—making sure everyone has a place to sit, with phone and Internet connections, with the lights turned on, and the AC or furnace working. All the details contribute to managing a facility complex. There are a lot of moving parts, a lot of i's to dot and t's to cross.

It's a somewhat thankless job. Like the cowboy, these folks work very hard. They have limited resources. They work a lot of overtime. And because they take pride in their work, they do it well. They may be the only ones

VOICE OF THE CUSTOMER

"IT JUST HAPPENS"

One of our customers spoke about the day-to-day details of the Facilities Team with the pride that marks these unsung professionals.

"My job is to provide creature comfort for our workers. Do I have the right ergonomic chair, the ergonomic desk? Is the air temperature correct? Is the facility being cleaned regularly? Is the trash being picked up?

"When I do my job right, people don't realize why everything is the way it is. We strive to make sure that, when you come in every day, the facility is at its highest quality. And I really mean that in every sense—the services—from delivering your mail, to cleaning your desk every night, to the elevators being polished and wiped down.

"There's a whole lot of stuff that we do. I think people appreciate it, but they don't think about it. They don't know why everything is the way it is; it just is. It just happens."

COWBOY HISTORY

WALTER AND ELLA FONDREN:
PRIMING THE PUMP WITH HARD WORK

Walter William Fondren drilled his first wells in search of water under the Arkansas farm his family had moved to from his native Tennessee. Orphaned at age 10, Walter worked in sawmills and on farms while still a boy. At 16, Walter moved along to Texas, where he used his knowledge of drilling as a roughneck in the Corsicana oilfield, the first major producer in Texas. Over the next four years, he learned rotary drilling and became an expert on drilling equipment.

All this hard work taught him the basics of producing oil and prepared him to move into the storied Spindletop oilfield. As an independent operator, he moved from field to field as new reservoirs of oil were discovered. Within a decade, he had accumulated enough wealth and expertise to join with others in raising the $150,000 capital to found the Humble Oil Company, which evolved into Exxon Company USA.

Like Walter, his wife, Ella, had grown up in a hardscrabble family that moved west—from Kentucky to Corsicana, Texas—seeking a better life. Ella was working in her family's boardinghouse when she met Walter, then just a roughneck. After they married, whenever Ella had a little leftover money from the household budget, she put it into stock for Texaco, Incorporated.

The Fondrens used the wealth they amassed to benefit the communities from which they had come. Their major gifts to medical institutions and universities included the Fondren libraries at Southern Methodist University and Rice University. Thus, the hardworking Fondrens left their mark not only on Houston but on many generations to come.

in the company who really understand what the work is and its impact on their end users and the bottom line. In many cases, senior management may not see a need to add support. (Remember our unsung hero?) In fact, in today's challenging economic times, Facilities Managers are frequently asked to cut expenses. And without good data, the Facilities Team has a tough time defending their budget and the value of the services they provide!

Workspace Cowboys desperately need the right tools. They need a better way to address the ongoing chores and the rapidly changing workplace. They need the proper foundation and architecture to capture the minutia while incorporating new dimensions such as mobile workers and shared space. At the same time, they don't want methods that add complication to what they already have on their plate. They want to keep things simple and get to the meat of the matter quickly. They need a partner that talks less and says more, whether it is a software application or the help desk that supports it.

WORKSPACE COWBOYS TACKLING THEIR CHORES

The following examples of three iOffice customers illustrate different Facilities Teams that had lots of moving parts. Let's see how these Workspace Cowboys tackled their chores.

Our first example comes from the major retailer we introduced when talking about the roundup (Code #2). At the time of its 25th anniversary, the company was experiencing

CONTEMPORARY BIZ

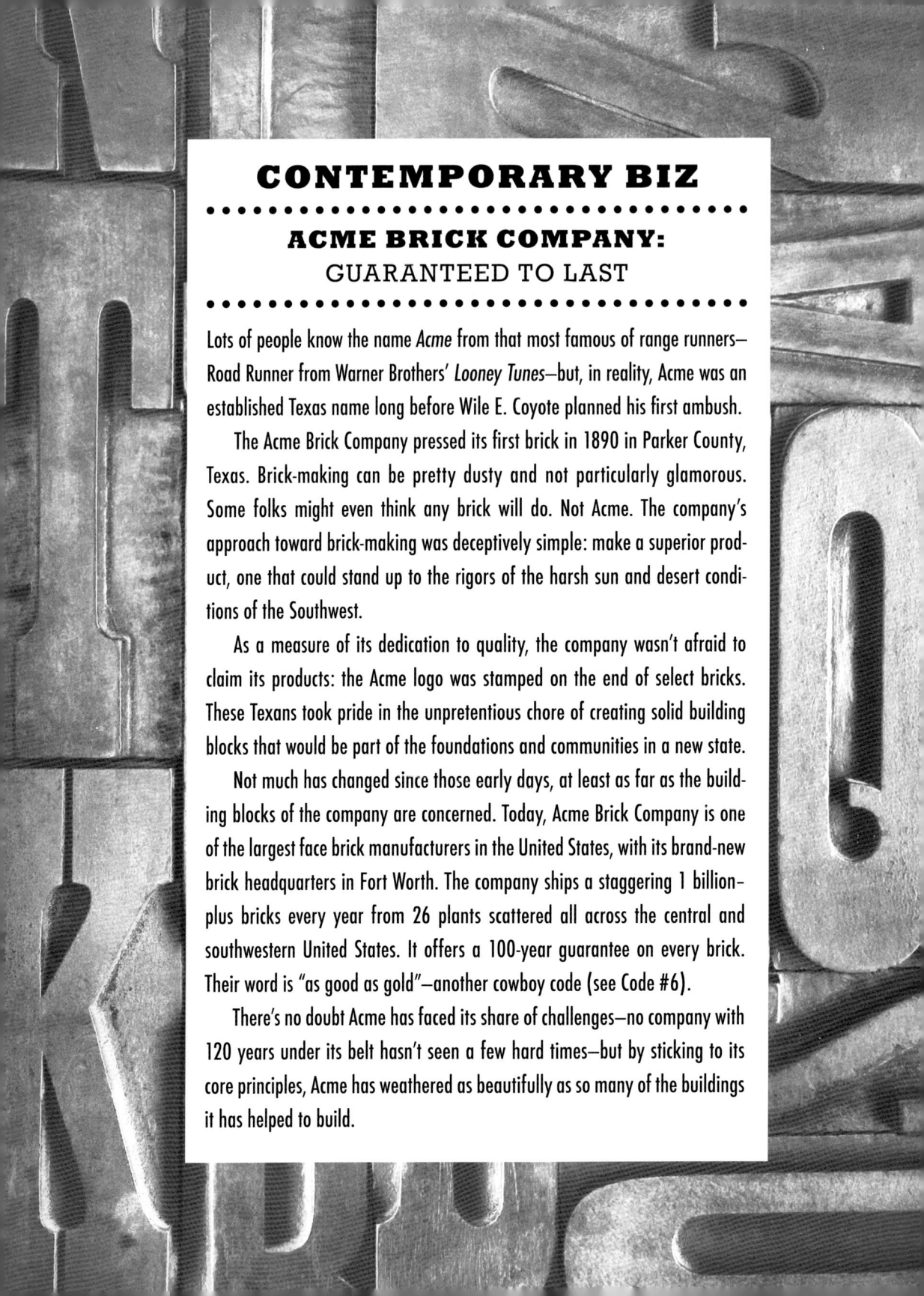

ACME BRICK COMPANY:
GUARANTEED TO LAST

Lots of people know the name *Acme* from that most famous of range runners—Road Runner from Warner Brothers' *Looney Tunes*—but, in reality, Acme was an established Texas name long before Wile E. Coyote planned his first ambush.

The Acme Brick Company pressed its first brick in 1890 in Parker County, Texas. Brick-making can be pretty dusty and not particularly glamorous. Some folks might even think any brick will do. Not Acme. The company's approach toward brick-making was deceptively simple: make a superior product, one that could stand up to the rigors of the harsh sun and desert conditions of the Southwest.

As a measure of its dedication to quality, the company wasn't afraid to claim its products: the Acme logo was stamped on the end of select bricks. These Texans took pride in the unpretentious chore of creating solid building blocks that would be part of the foundations and communities in a new state.

Not much has changed since those early days, at least as far as the building blocks of the company are concerned. Today, Acme Brick Company is one of the largest face brick manufacturers in the United States, with its brand-new brick headquarters in Fort Worth. The company ships a staggering 1 billion-plus bricks every year from 26 plants scattered all across the central and southwestern United States. It offers a 100-year guarantee on every brick. Their word is "as good as gold"—another cowboy code (see Code #6).

There's no doubt Acme has faced its share of challenges—no company with 120 years under its belt hasn't seen a few hard times—but by sticking to its core principles, Acme has weathered as beautifully as so many of the buildings it has helped to build.

rapid growth through new stores, additional distribution centers, new services for businesses and consumers, and international expansion. With a workforce of more than 300,000 associates, the retailer's growth generated about 200 employee moves per month, just at the company headquarters (due to new hires, promotions, reorganizations, etc.).

At that time, the company had essentially no process to move employees and the related assets. Workers changing their office locations coordinated their own moves. For example, the moving employee would call IT, call the furniture vendor, and contact the phone company directly—a process requiring two or three days of the employee's time.

WORKSPACE COWBOYS DESPERATELY NEED **THE RIGHT TOOLS.** THEY NEED A BETTER WAY TO ADDRESS THE ONGOING CHORES AND THE **RAPIDLY CHANGING WORKPLACE.** THEY NEED THE PROPER FOUNDATION AND ARCHITECTURE TO CAPTURE THE MINUTIA WHILE INCORPORATING **NEW DIMENSIONS** SUCH AS MOBILE WORKERS AND SHARED SPACE.

By implementing the Space Management Module of the iOffice platform, the Corporate & Facilities Services Representative transformed the employee move process. Physical inventory, floor plans, cubicle and occupant information, and phone and data jacks were all loaded into the program. That basic information allowed the company to begin using the Move/Add/Change functions to effectively coordinate a move at a significant cost savings. Today, the employee submits a move request, it is approved on-line, and all the vendors and services are scheduled automatically. Meanwhile, the employee in transition is free to do his or her primary job.

Before the iOffice platform, this retailer could not enforce its policies relating to office locations and the amount of space assigned. No centralized database defined the nature or location of the space occupied by the workers. Without such a directory, support functions had to search the floor to deliver a package or provide IT support. Now, the Facilities Team applies space, furniture, and equipment parameters to each job title and function. When a move request is submitted, the appropriate standards are applied. For example, a vice president receives an office with a certain amount of square feet, while an administrative assistant has a workstation with a smaller space allocation. Real-time data allows the Facilities Team to quickly determine and make efficient use of available space. The iOffice tool has helped reduce and even eliminate leases for new space.

The Facilities Representatives at this major retailer transformed a costly, ad hoc process into a professionally managed one; they turned the "mundane chore" of an employee move into an opportunity to add value to the worker being moved, his or her department, the vendors supporting the move, and the shareholders. Focused on the right details, these Workspace Cowboys saved their company over $1 million per year.

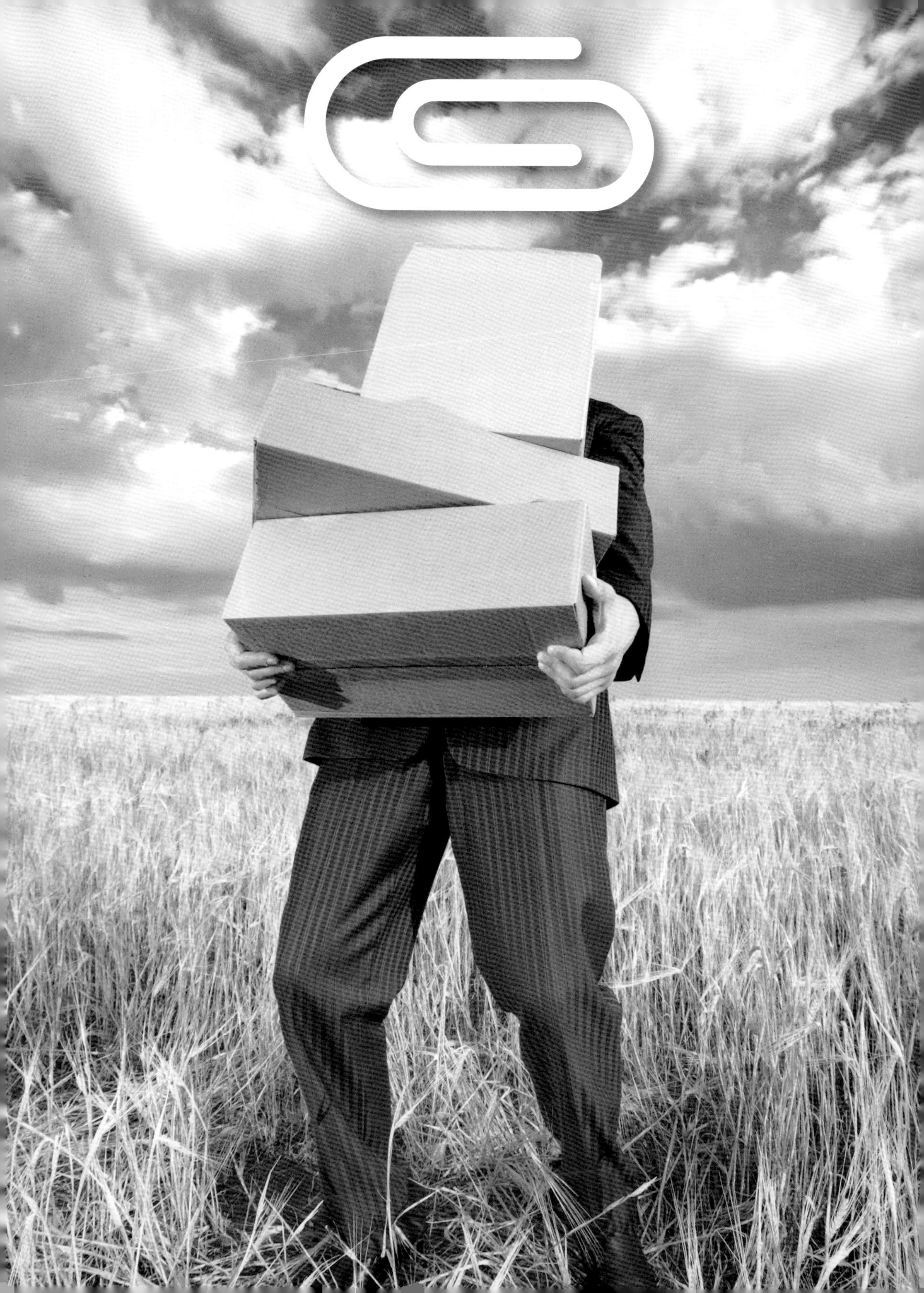

WIDE OPEN WORKSPACE

IN OUR DISCUSSION of Code #1, one of the trailblazers was a major healthcare network. A few years ago, that corporation moved its headquarters from scattered office locations to a brand-new building. As the move got underway, the Corporate & Facilities Services Representative realized that the internal and external resources designated to support the move could not handle the "chores." The whole herd was in jeopardy.

The tool that the company had planned to use to track the move was the Property Manager's software for routine maintenance requests. However, that tool was not up to the complexity and scope of the headquarters move; for example, there was no way to manage locks and keys, or keep track of shredders. Furthermore, there was no tool to manage space and office utilization in the new building. With Excel spreadsheets, it was not only difficult to validate what space was occupied and by whom, but the existing tool created time-consuming work for the Facilities staff. Finally, there was no means to measure the level of service and cost of the activities performed by the Facilities Team.

At the request of this healthcare network, iOffice stepped in. We verified all assets and office contents at the location of origin, ensuring they were accurately identified and labeled on the master move list. As items were received at the new location, iOffice again verified accuracy of assets and office contents actually delivered to their final location. Because these chores were completed successfully, the Corporate & Facilities Services Representative asked iOffice to design a specific plan to meet the specialized needs of the Executive

Suite. By efficiently managing the details, that move was completed successfully as well.

While working on the not-so-glamorous chores related to the move,* iOffice earned the opportunity to introduce its platform to the healthcare corporation. Today, this company is utilizing a full suite of iOffice services at their headquarters location. With it, they manage maintenance requests, track services, manage space, coordinate moves, register visitors, and track mail. Easy to use and full-service, the iOffice platform is becoming the tool for managing all of the company's clinics across the country.

What started as a moving nightmare became an opportunity for the Facilities Team to shine. What happens behind the scenes affects performance on the front lines. By getting the details right, these Workspace Cowboys are an integral part of this healthcare network's outstanding reputation.

LET'S REVISIT THE global energy company you met in our discussion of the roundup (Code #2). About five years ago, a new Corporate & Facilities Services Representative was given the goal of providing a standard level of service across all of the corporation's locations in over 20 countries. The objective was to give employees the same level of experience when engaging facility services anywhere in the world (i.e., to do the chores well everywhere).

To accomplish this, the Facilities staff was reorganized as a centralized team with a global reach. At the start, they had

---

* iOffice no longer offers the service of physically assisting clients in their moves. We exited that business in 2011 to place our complete focus on software.

VOICE OF THE CUSTOMER

THE VANISHING FILE ROOM

One client, who works at a company that provides imaging and print solutions, shared his view on how the move to be paperless is changing the nature of one important chore—the keeping of company records.

"The move to be 'paperless' can be found in manufacturing plants, distribution, and back office processes. Industries that are going paperless include healthcare, higher education, legal, financial, retail, technology firms, and manufacturing.

"Let's visit a file room in a legal firm. When working on an active case, lawyers use a lot of files from previous trials. In the past, the manila folder or binders went back and forth. Sometimes attorneys could not find the material they needed for handling a time-sensitive case.

"Now, there is an electronic solution. It's as easy as putting a barcode on a file folder and then checking file folders in and out of the storage area. Scanning the barcode keeps track of who has each file. Attorney Thurber can send an email request: 'I need file folder 1234.' The person tending the file cage can grab the needed file folder, scan it, and then identify that Thurber picked up the file on such and such a date. If somebody else comes looking for that file folder, the file room knows Thurber has it and can ask, 'Are you done with the file? We need to check it back in so we can check it out to somebody else.' Many public libraries are installing this type of system for their books and audiovisual materials.

"The barcodes are just a first step. Today, we've got all these file cabinets full of paper. However, it is possible to scan all those documents, create a digital file, and put that out in the cloud. When people can access the documents in the cloud, the file room will disappear."

just voicemail, email, and spreadsheets as their management tools. At headquarters alone, the team was managing ten floors of space and serving over 1,500 employees. Although responding to service requests, they could not track the type or volume of services, nor the time required to deliver them. They could not measure the quality or cost of the services provided. Furthermore, they lacked reliable information to make accurate decisions about resources required throughout the company.

WHAT HAPPENS BEHIND THE SCENES AFFECTS PERFORMANCE ON THE FRONT LINES. BY GETTING THE DETAILS RIGHT, THESE WORKSPACE COWBOYS ARE AN INTEGRAL PART OF THIS HEALTHCARE NETWORK'S OUTSTANDING REPUTATION.

This global company chose the iOffice platform as the tool to help them achieve their objectives. The cloud-based software automated all of the manual processes used to receive, dispatch, and track service requests. It allowed the Corporate & Facilities Services Team to view and measure the types and levels of services they were delivering. It allowed the office floor plans to be published on-line. In addition, the tool allowed the Facilities Team to plan move scenarios and track changes during a move, with real-time updates of floor plans. As a result, the company's senior managers were able to understand actual space use and cost.

The global company began implementing the tool at the Texas location and is now expanding its use to other sites, including one of its principal offices in the Northeast.

Because the iOffice tool is cloud based and easily configured, additional offices can be added within the same database. Each location can operate independently but be managed centrally to support the global facility standard that this leader hopes to achieve.

iOFFICE AND WORKSPACE CHORES

These customer examples illustrate how the iOffice portal embraces all those mundane activities, all those moving parts, all those employees. It helps you manage your herd and lets you work from any location.

Also, because the iOffice platform is modular, a company can begin with the basic foundations and then expand, as the company changes. By using a tool that leverages his or her time and team, the Workspace Cowboy can take care of the detailed chores, but also have the means to look ahead and plan how to use physical resources to benefit the human resources and the shareholders. We hope our solutions make our customers proud—proud for keeping up with their chores and proud for keeping up with the times.

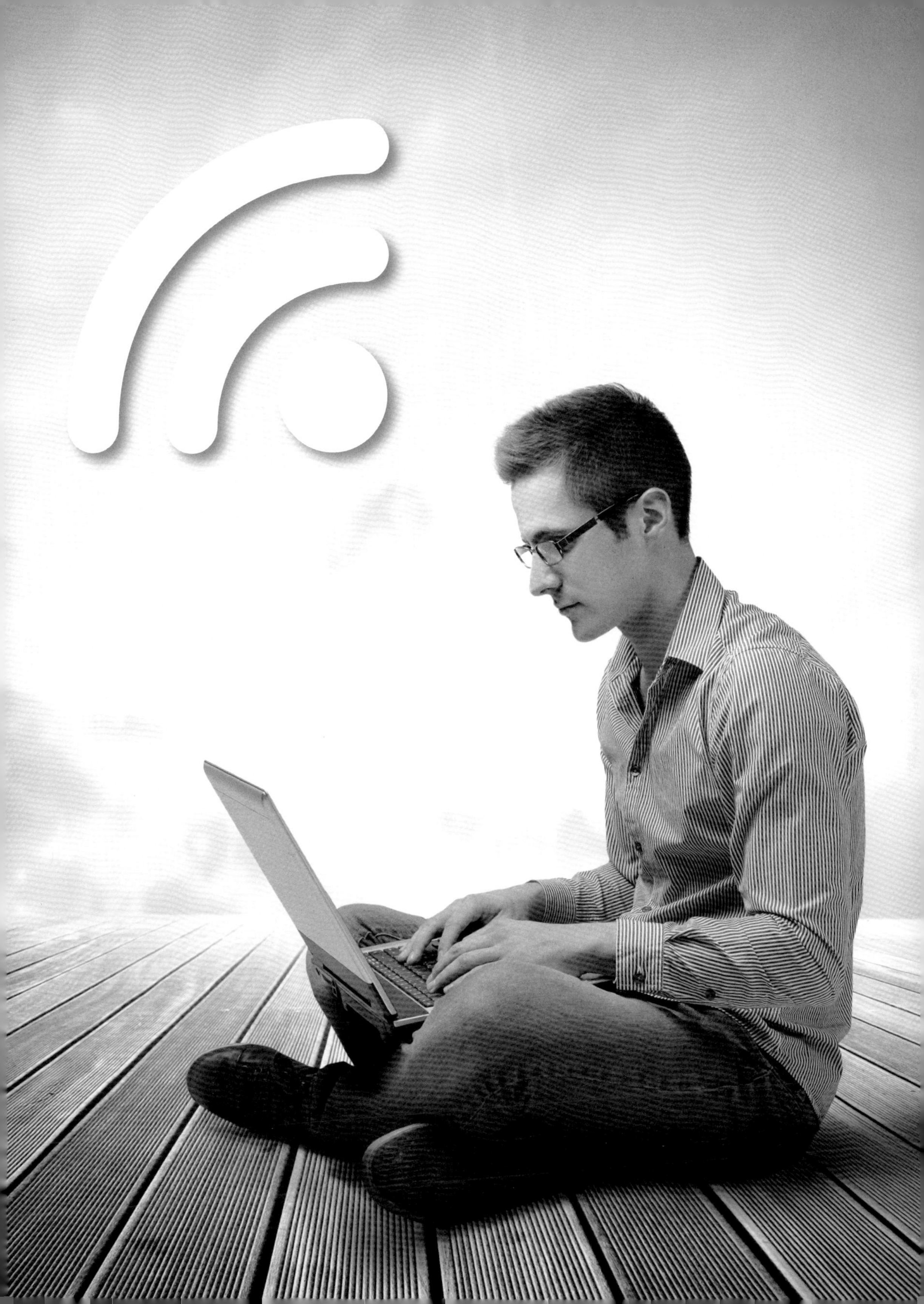

SIMPLE

CODE #5: COWBOYS KEEP AN EYE OUT FOR WHAT WORKS

WHETHER TENDING TO chores or imagining the future, the Facilities Team has a full plate. Although we have already touched on the importance of something simple that works, we would like to elaborate on that theme with this code that was central to the cowboy's creed.

With his horse as his home, a cowboy had to choose his tools carefully and make them serve more than one purpose. The saddle was not just a comfortable seat; it had a projection called a "horn" that could grab the rope if he needed an extra hand. The ten-gallon hat that protected him from the sun also scooped up water to ease a thirst.

Cowboys kept it simple. They had to, and they always kept an eye out for what worked. There was no shame in learning from others and borrowing good ideas. In fact, the cowboys' skills and methods came from diverse cultures—postwar soldiers, Native Americans, former slaves, newcomers from Europe. A good idea was welcome from anywhere, and trail mates often came together from far-flung places.

FINDING WHAT WORKS IN THE WORKSPACE ARENA

In today's age of bells and whistles, simplicity is still an important value in business, especially in the world of facilities management. We have already seen the potential scope of the job, ranging from turning on the lights to turning on the talent pool. Easy-to-use tools are a must.

However, we have also mentioned the diverse and unique circumstances of each organization. Job titles are just a hint of that diversity. Different industries have different requirements. Consider the contrasts between a healthcare facility, a major retailer, a technology start-up, and a university campus. Of course, within an industry there can also be a great variance. As an example, let's zoom in on healthcare: a small community clinic has very different challenges from a multi-building medical campus. Therefore, the Workspace Cowboy wants something simple, but also something that fits his organization's specific situation—just as a cowboy wants his own saddle to fit him just right.

Workspace Cowboys look for simplicity, customization, and adaptability. As companies grow, relocate, or shift strategic focus, their facilities must expand, be reconfigured, or contract. The Facilities Manager needs tools that are flexible and can evolve to meet all those challenges. We see this in the following couple of iOffice customers who keep an eye out for what works.

With operations in over 30 countries, a global software company helps its customers simplify processes and workflow. Consistent with the company's hallmark of providing

VOICE OF THE CUSTOMER

EFFICIENCY IN A CORPORATE TURNAROUND

An interview with CEO Philip Flynn was published recently in which he spoke about working on diverse fronts to reverse the financial results of Associated Bank. As a provider to the bank, we were proud to see the importance he placed on technology solutions.

"So you do have to focus on being more efficient. In our case, we are not particularly efficient. The company over the years prior to me coming here did not reinvest appropriately into the franchise. So some of what we've had to do is catch up, investing in technology solutions so we can get more efficient and do things in a less manual way.

"We have an imperative to become more efficient. Most of our expenses are people related. So we are trying to figure out a way, particularly now in the processing areas and back shops, to get more efficient with technology solutions. And that's a long process."

VOICE OF THE CUSTOMER

MAKING IT WORK TODAY AND IN THE FUTURE

The following comments were made by a Facilities Representative in a dynamic company that moves about 50 employees per month.

"As we configure space for today, we need to think about the way the company runs its business. In two years, many of the business teams will need to move somewhere else.

"When one team moves, I've got to put somebody else in whatever space they leave behind. So I have to think, 'Does it fit them today? Does it fit their purpose?' But, I'm careful about how I 'fit for purpose,' knowing that, later, I will need to transition the area into something else.

"So I look at how I'm going to house the team today. I imagine how I can make their stay as comfortable and as engaging as possible, knowing that in two years I'll probably move them again. I keep one eye on the future and ask, 'How am I going to use this space later?'

"When I do a construction project, I don't just put walls up because I've got to get it done. I ask, 'What other group can I fit in here that would want this same type of setup?' Therefore, I won't build something I know is a one-off that we'll never use again.

"Let's say that a group needs a project room, and they need it right in the middle of their workspace. That's a tough one because not everybody needs a project room. I will ask them, 'Could we take down one of the collaboration rooms and make that your project room? Could we take half of a file room and make it into a project room?' I'm not trying to deny them a project room, but I will try to see if we can retrofit something we already have. We take it department by department and really look at what they're trying to do. We explore options to create the space they need in a cost-effective way while giving some thought to the longer term."

simple, workable solutions, the Corporate & Facilities Services Representatives do the same for the workspace.

Rapid growth and a dynamic workforce posed the need to relocate employees and physical assets (e.g., equipment, furnishings) in a timely, efficient manner. To address this challenge, the software company turned first to one of its own products, an application that allowed employees to submit move requests. However, the existing tool provided only a partial solution. Once the request was received, the move had to be coordinated manually between task groups. For example, Facilities scheduled the move of furniture and files, while IT scheduled the setup of computer workstations.

COWBOYS KEPT IT SIMPLE. THEY HAD TO, AND THEY ALWAYS KEPT AN EYE OUT FOR WHAT WORKED.

Needing a more effective solution, the software company worked with iOffice to create an interface between their existing software and the iOffice platform, namely the Move Management and Space Management modules.

Once the solution was implemented, the workforce could still submit their move requests as before, the way they were used to, but the interface automatically created move tickets. This allowed our customer's management team to coordinate, track, and approve moves in an automated way that saved money and time. The software also allowed floor plans to be seamlessly updated so that management could understand real-time use and prepare properly for changing needs.

CONTEMPORARY BIZ

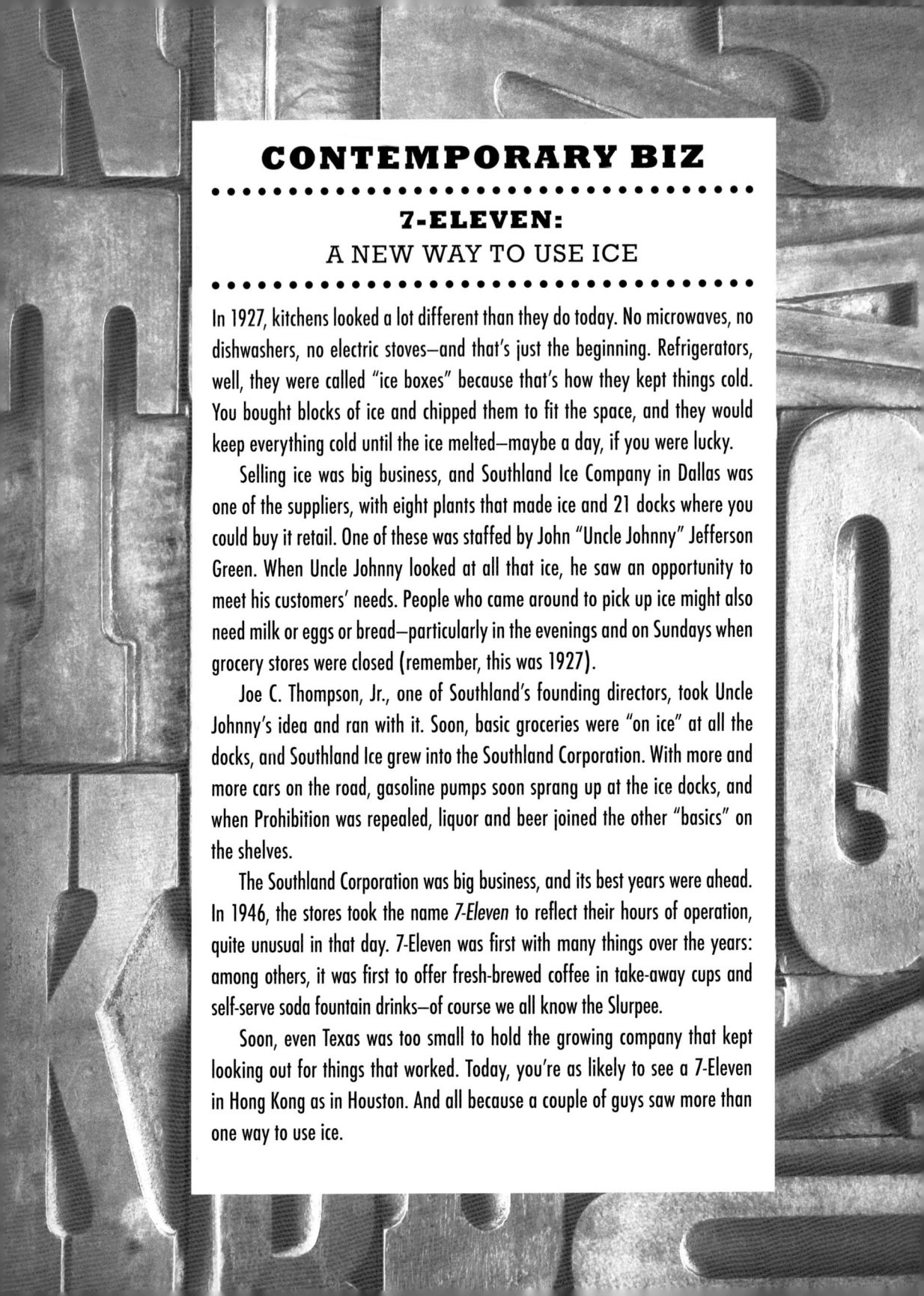

7-ELEVEN:
A NEW WAY TO USE ICE

In 1927, kitchens looked a lot different than they do today. No microwaves, no dishwashers, no electric stoves—and that's just the beginning. Refrigerators, well, they were called "ice boxes" because that's how they kept things cold. You bought blocks of ice and chipped them to fit the space, and they would keep everything cold until the ice melted—maybe a day, if you were lucky.

Selling ice was big business, and Southland Ice Company in Dallas was one of the suppliers, with eight plants that made ice and 21 docks where you could buy it retail. One of these was staffed by John "Uncle Johnny" Jefferson Green. When Uncle Johnny looked at all that ice, he saw an opportunity to meet his customers' needs. People who came around to pick up ice might also need milk or eggs or bread—particularly in the evenings and on Sundays when grocery stores were closed (remember, this was 1927).

Joe C. Thompson, Jr., one of Southland's founding directors, took Uncle Johnny's idea and ran with it. Soon, basic groceries were "on ice" at all the docks, and Southland Ice grew into the Southland Corporation. With more and more cars on the road, gasoline pumps soon sprang up at the ice docks, and when Prohibition was repealed, liquor and beer joined the other "basics" on the shelves.

The Southland Corporation was big business, and its best years were ahead. In 1946, the stores took the name *7-Eleven* to reflect their hours of operation, quite unusual in that day. 7-Eleven was first with many things over the years: among others, it was first to offer fresh-brewed coffee in take-away cups and self-serve soda fountain drinks—of course we all know the Slurpee.

Soon, even Texas was too small to hold the growing company that kept looking out for things that worked. Today, you're as likely to see a 7-Eleven in Hong Kong as in Houston. And all because a couple of guys saw more than one way to use ice.

These Workspace Cowboys "kept an eye out for what works." Rather than reinvent the wheel, they adopted existing software, a tool from their own product set. Next, when more functionality was needed, they sought out a partner, iOffice, who could adapt and improve something that was already working for the software company's employees.

IN THE PREVIOUS chapter, we learned how a healthcare network executed a complex headquarters move by "taking pride in their chores" and finding a technology platform that would support the transition. The Corporate & Facilities Services Representative at that company likes to keep things simple. To him, it made no sense to use 15-plus software systems to manage the locations of the parent company. *"Those systems have lots of bells and whistles, many of which were never installed,"* he explained. *"iOffice provides a simple, easy-to-use solution."*

iOffice continues building its relationship with this healthcare network to meet the company's ongoing needs. From product design to pricing, we try to build on what works. For example, we have modified our product for the smaller clinics in the network. The result is a solution that is easy to use, reasonable in cost, and consistent across the entire organization.

Here is how the Corporate & Facilities Services Representative views the change.

> *Prior to iOffice, we did not have a way to view space utilization real-time across multiple buildings. We did not have an efficient planning tool for moves;*

we could not identify spaces by type. The iOffice tool has given the occupants of all buildings within the network and its parent company the ability to view assets, look at room configurations, and easily find where an employee is based. These tools along with all the other pieces of the facility management platform (such as service requests and mail center operations) provide a comprehensive one-stop shop for us.

iOFFICE VALUES SIMPLE THINGS THAT WORK

A lot of Workspace Cowboys choose iOffice because our product is simple, even though it does complex things. The software is easy to use, easy to implement, and intuitive. We expressly designed it that way. The Facilities Manager does not have to hire extra people and send them offsite for several days in order to study a three-ring binder about how the application works.

Implementing a platform like this one can be intimidating. Many of our customers didn't grow up in the Digital Age. They want software that can be up and running quickly, without a lot of training. They appreciate something that is easy to understand and won't make them look foolish. They need an investment from which they can get a return quickly, without a big cost burden.

Our business model is adaptive and we install quickly. We have a standardized plan and we have a methodology that makes it as seamless as possible. Most importantly, it's fluid. If the business process changes in six months, our users can reconfigure the modules to fit their new

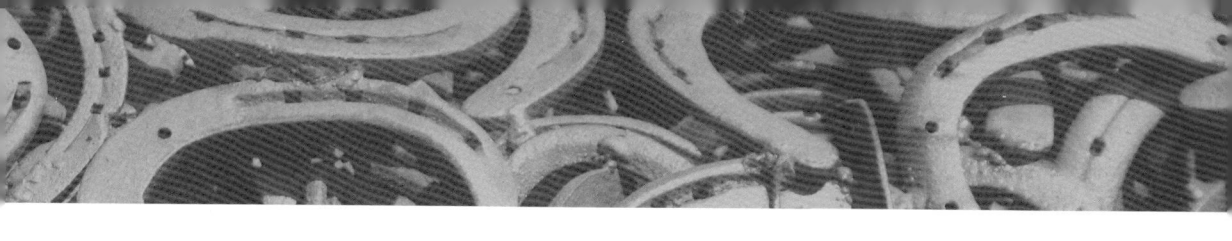

COWBOY HISTORY

NO-FRILLS FOOTWEAR:
THE EVOLUTION OF THE COWBOY BOOT

Call 'em "kicks" or "roach stompers," there's no mistaking the trademark footwear of the cowboy: the pointy-toed, calf-high leather boot, whether it's butter-soft and done up with fancy stitching or tough and covered with the muck and dust of the trail.

The cowboy boot had a purely pragmatic beginning. Fact was, when the Civil War ended and the cattle trade really took off in Texas, there wasn't a good riding boot. Many of the men riding the trails in those days were former soldiers, just back from the war (and from both sides of the Mason-Dixon Line). They had spent the war in heavy army boots that were made for marching and protecting the feet from the elements. But these low-riding, wide-soled boots had all kinds of problems when it came to spending a day on horseback and working with cattle.

As the story goes, a few years after the war ended, an enterprising cowboy took his boots to a cobbler and asked for a redesign. (Depending on whom you believe, this happened in either Kansas, another major cattle state, or Texas, but no one seriously disputes that cowboy boots are synonymous with Texas nowadays.) This cowboy had a few particular ideas about his ideal riding boot. First, it had to be easy to get into stirrups, so it needed a pointed toe. Second, it had to protect the ankle and calf from chafing in the stirrup and from the many hazards of the trail, including rattlesnakes, so it needed to be constructed from tough leather that went at least partway up the leg. Finally, it had to give some purchase on the trail and, in the event of a spooked horse, stop the cowboy's foot from sliding completely through the stirrup, leaving him hung up and hurt. Hence, the high wooden heel.

These first cowboy boots weren't much to look at, but they got the job done. The stitching was utilitarian, and lots of the early models had loops on the top so they could be pulled up quick (like the boots of firemen). But pretty or not, other riders knew a good idea when they saw it, and soon specially made cowboy boots were in high demand. In the early years, each pair was custom-made.

Over time, of course, cowboy boots traveled far off the cattle trail and outside of Texas, and as they did, they transformed from the utilitarian working boot of a hard-riding cowboy to a fashion statement that would forever be wedded to the Lone Star State. But even in the fanciest dress boot, there's still an echo of the hard trails where the cowboy boot was born.

VOICE OF THE CUSTOMER

MAKING IT WORK WITH A KIT OF PARTS

Cowboys traveled light, with a few basics that worked. Each cowboy had his own boots, his own hat, and his own saddle—universal gear that was modified to fit each rider. One iOffice customer has a similar approach to its facilities design.

"Even within a company, not all locations are alike and not all people work the same way. So, we've developed a kit of parts—a standard size of furniture and offices, color palettes, those types of things.

"One of the items in the kit of parts is the 'touchdown space.' Before the renovation we had a 16-seat visitor mobility center, where people could drop down if they came in from another location, but they were siphoned off from the rest of the campus. The current touchdowns are incorporated into each floor, along with workstations and private offices.

"We're experimenting with a 'travel office.' If someone is in the office less than 50 percent of the time, they have an office that is theirs when they are here, but when they are not here, it can be used as a huddle room. However, we do not draw a line in the sand and say every single location's going to look alike, because that's not going to be the case. Things need to change a little bit from location to location."

requirements. We try to make them heroes through flexibility, configurability, and having the information they need at their fingertips.

The product architecture and design are based on the tenets of simplicity, ease of use, and flexibility. Every module has the same format and operates in the same way. Every module has a queue-based form or a list of services, with icons and graphics that lead you where you need to go. Even the overall look and feel puts the user at ease; it's icon driven, with minimal words.

Built on a simple hierarchy, the services are all formatted in the same way. Users can add a menu of service requests very intuitively. For example, if they are building a catalog of requests for heating and air conditioning services, they can enter choices for their workers to select, such as, "It's too hot," "It's too cold," or "The air vent is broken."

WORKSPACE COWBOYS NEED SIMPLE TOOLS THAT ARE EASY TO GET UP AND RUNNING, TOOLS THAT ENHANCE PRODUCTIVITY IN THEIR OWN DEPARTMENT AND IN THE ENTIRE WORKFORCE.

The iOffice platform is modular, so users can choose the services that meet their business needs. For instance, if they want to manage floor plans but not service requests, they can activate just the module they need through the portal. Users don't activate or pay for modules they don't want. Here's another example: The OpenSpace application allows employees to search for and reserve office spaces

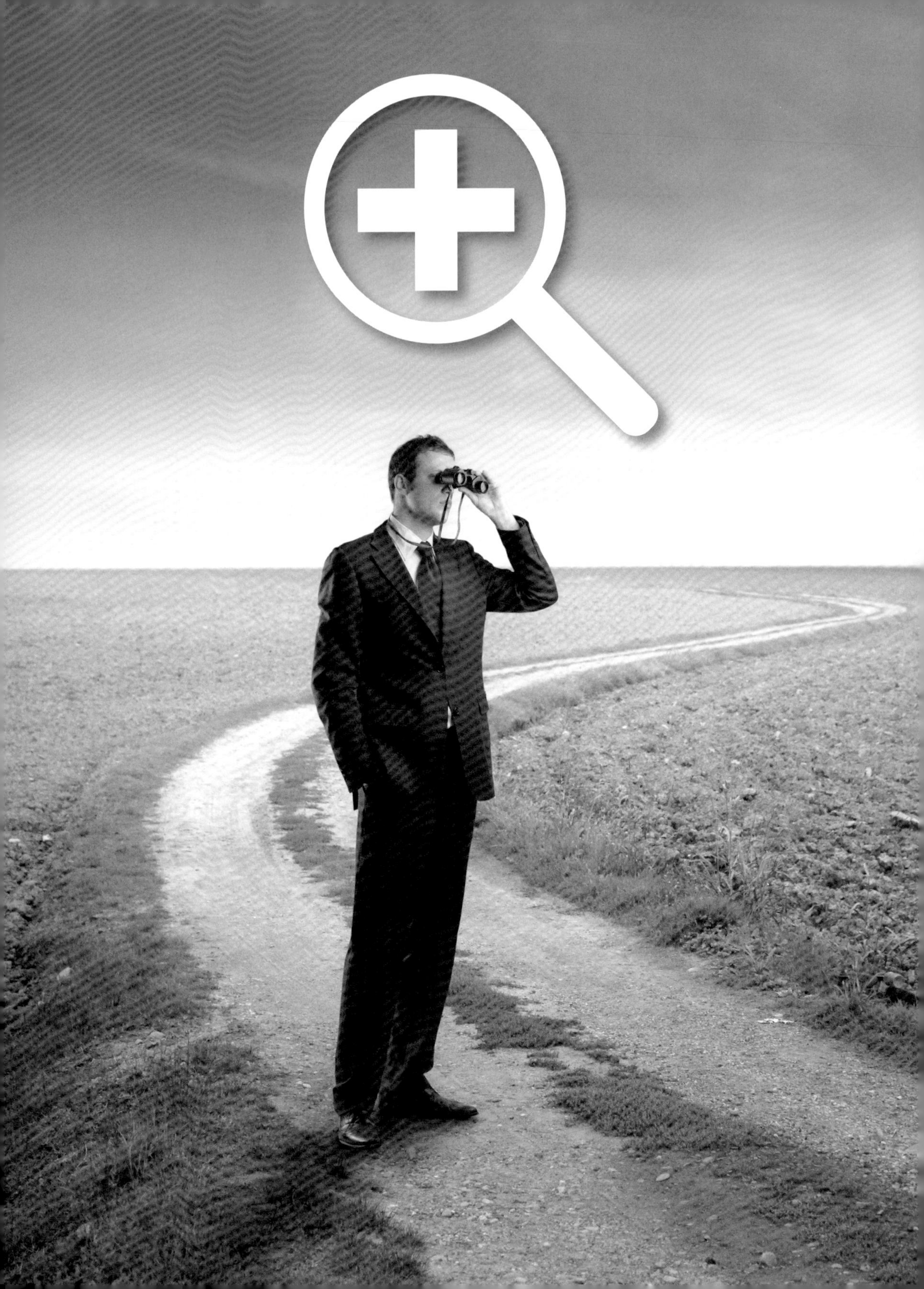

and conference rooms. All that is required is a reservation list, without any floor plans. A company can activate and pay for just that functionality.

Facilities Managers can control and customize the software. For example, the ability to automatically send email notifications about service status can be toggled on or off. The fields and information in each module can be modified to fit the company environment and workflow. Like the saddle of a cowboy, the software is attuned to the specific role of the Facilities Manager. That lets him focus on his herd, the people he services. Having the right information at his fingertips allows him to make good, proactive business decisions—for individual employees and for the company as a whole.

Cowboys have no use for things that don't work. Facilities Managers are busy people managing a very dynamic environment. Workspace Cowboys need simple tools that are easy to get up and running, tools that enhance productivity in their own department and in the entire workforce. At iOffice we aim to deliver just that.

TRUST

CODE #6: A COWBOY'S WORD IS AS GOOD AS GOLD

TODAY'S WORKPLACE IS cluttered with rules and regulations. Too often, rules are seen as something to "get around," rather than as valuable guides for conduct. Most people sign unread documents or click the *Accept* button, rather than wade through the pages of legalese that accompany many transactions. Litigation, rather than conversation, has become the norm for conflict resolution. The business world sometimes feels like the Wild West, with every person out for his or her own interests. In this context, trust has emerged as the glue that binds relationships together, just as it did on the open range.

There were no laws on the prairie, so cowboys had to trust one another to keep agreements and promises. Contracts were often verbal, and a handshake was the only signature. But a cowboy's word was a rock-solid guarantee.

Charles Goodnight, a Texas cowboy before the Civil War, is one example. A trailblazer, Goodnight invented the chuck wagon and carved out a new route to Kansas. With his partner, Oliver Loving, he drove feral Texas cattle to the railroads on what became known as the Goodnight-Loving Trail. When Loving died, Goodnight kept a deathbed promise to return his partner's body from New Mexico to Weatherford, Texas, for burial. His word was as good as gold.

Trust breeds trust. Oliver Loving had a trail driver named Bose Ikard, who became Goodnight's new partner. Ikard was a freed black slave whom Goodnight said he trusted "farther than any living man. He was my detective, banker, and everything else."

TRUST IN THE WORKSPACE ARENA

Workspace Cowboys are committed to delivering a high level of service and following through with their commitments to their customers. They are good stewards of physical assets and get the chores done as promised. With the evolution of the workspace, companies are placing additional trust in their Facilities Teams—trust that Facilities will enable the success of the workers through new methods.

We trust people who deliver, and mistrust those who don't. Being able to fulfill promises in the work world requires having the tools and skillsets necessary to do the job. When operations are in flux, trailblazing and innovating (Code #1) are the name of the game. Reaching out to a partner, as Goodnight did to Ikard, may also contribute to solutions. And, as illustrated by the trio of Goodnight, Loving, and Ikard, those partnerships may radiate out, like concentric circles. The following example reflects

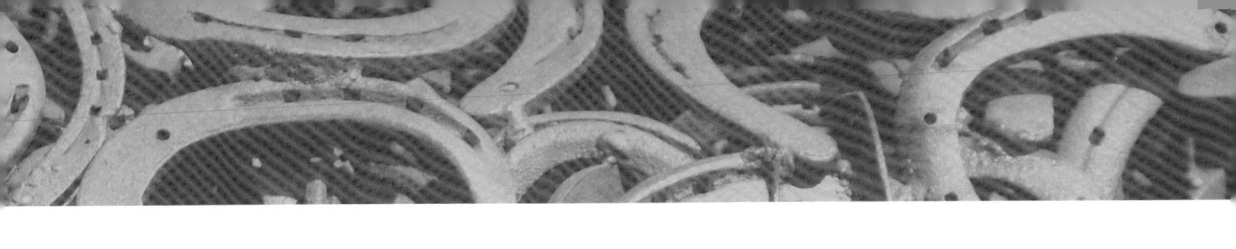

COWBOY HISTORY

STEPHEN AUSTIN:
A TEXAS-SIZED PROMISE

Stephen Austin is recognized today as one of the founding fathers of Texas, but who knows what would have happened if not for a promise Austin made to his own father, Moses.

Stephen Austin was born in 1793 in Virginia and then moved with his family at the age of 5 to Missouri, where Moses worked in the metals business. At age 10, Stephen was sent back East to school in Connecticut, and then to university in Kentucky. When he returned to Missouri at the age of 17, he took over his family's store and started a promising career in politics and land speculation. Stephen served in the Missouri militia and worked as a territorial legislator. By 1820, he had moved to Arkansas, where he served as a circuit judge and bought and sold land. None of this had much to do with Texas, and that was probably fine with the man who would eventually lend his name to the Texas state capital.

But destiny had other things in mind for young Stephen Austin. While he was making a name for himself in Arkansas, his father was traveling to San Antonio, which was then in the Spanish-controlled territory of Mexico. Moses obtained permission from the Spanish crown to settle 300 American families in the Texas territory. After he obtained permission to start up a colony, he appealed to his son to join him in the Texas venture. Historical records are clear that Stephen Austin wasn't enthusiastic, but he agreed to go along with Moses's plan.

By then, Stephen was an enterprising businessman in his own right. He helped arrange financing for the project and traveled to Nacogdoches (now a town in Texas near the Louisiana border) to meet his father and launch the enterprise. That's where he learned of his father's death.

One wonders what thoughts went through Austin's mind at that crucial time. The idea of Texas had yet to take hold in his imagination; this was his father's grant, his father's deal. True, Stephen had borrowed money to make it possible, but there was still time for him to walk away with his honor intact.

Of course, that's not what he did. Stephen decided to honor his father's dream and the agreement he'd made with his father to turn that dream into a reality. Austin traveled on to San Antonio, where he received permission from the regional governor, Antonio Maria Martinez, to continue the project on his own. Armed with this assurance, Austin traveled to New Orleans, where he put out notice that land was up for grabs in the Texas territory and set the wheels in motion for the State of Texas to be born.

CONTEMPORARY BIZ

WHOLE FOODS MARKET:
KEEPING GMOs TRANSPARENT

In today's complicated world, it can sometimes feel like there's no such thing as a "conversation" about what people should be eating and what's safe. From no-carb diets to exotic supplements, it seems like everybody has an opinion—and it's only the bravest of companies that take a stand one way or the other.

Texas-based Whole Foods Market became one of those companies in early 2013. The company's top executives made a promise to consumers: within five years, all Whole Foods products will be labeled to indicate whether or not they contain genetically modified organisms, known as GMOs. In making this promise, Whole Foods Market became the first nationwide grocery store to tackle this complicated issue.

There's no shortage of controversy when it comes to GMO foods, in part because they are so prevalent. According to the Non-GMO Project, around 90 percent of soy, corn, cotton, and beets planted in the United States are GMO crops, meaning that the vast majority of processed foods contain some GMO ingredients.

The debate over the health effects of GMO foods is heated and emotional. According to the U.S. Food and Drug Administration, dozens of GMO crops have been approved for planting and sale because they pose no known health risks. Overseas, however, more than 60 countries have either instituted GMO labeling laws or restricted GMO crops outright. Meanwhile, a raging debate has consumed much of the nutrition world, with groups lining up for and against GMO labeling and planting.

In making a bold promise to forge ahead with "GMO transparency," Whole Foods Market has made a promise to provide its customers with choices, despite the challenges of sourcing non-GMO products.

a partnership of mutual trust that has existed for more than a decade.

One of our customers, a leader in imaging and print solutions, did not have a technology platform to accurately track and measure the service improvements it was implementing for its clients. Paper logs and spreadsheets were being used to record activities, performance, and costs. In addition to being unwieldy and prone to errors, this process consumed a lot of time. Someone had to summarize and consolidate data from diverse sources to create monthly reports. However, the biggest cost was the loss of customers due to the fact that the company could not measure results and demonstrate how its services were saving money for its clients.

BEING ABLE TO FULFILL PROMISES IN THE WORK WORLD REQUIRES HAVING THE TOOLS AND SKILLSETS NECESSARY TO DO THE JOB.

This company turned to iOffice to address these issues, in part because we offered a solution that was delivered via the web, known in the industry as a SaaS ("software as a service") solution. The software and data storage are in the cloud; the client company does not have to install software on its computer or dedicate IT time to supporting the programs.

By working with iOffice, our customer was able to

- **Eliminate paper logs and Excel spreadsheets.** All service requests are submitted, tracked, and measured through the iOffice platform.

- **Develop real-time reports.** iOffice provides both the imaging company and its customers with real-time reporting information. The most current activities, performance ratings, and costs can be reviewed simultaneously by the service provider and the customer.

- **Eliminate multiple, disparate systems.** The iOffice software allows our customer to manage each location and its unique requirements through a single system.

- **Create and implement operational standards for service delivery.** Because tools are standardized and configured across all locations, operational teams can work seamlessly between multiple sites using the same standards.

- **Significantly minimize the company's IT involvement and, therefore, IT costs.**

- **Enhance the value it delivers to its customers.** The iOffice software offers not only copy, mail, and copier fleet management services, but also space management and planning, visitor tracking, document and asset tracking, and maintenance request management.

THE iOFFICE PORTAL ALLOWS THIS COMPANY TO KEEP ITS COMMITMENTS AND "STAND BEHIND ITS WORD."

With the cloud-based iOffice platform in place, this global enterprise is able to serve thousands of customers with a consistent level of excellence, even when the customers' operations are dispersed geographically. Consistently delivering on commitments builds trust for the vendor with its

VOICE OF THE CUSTOMER

BUILDING TRUST BY DELIVERING AS PROMISED

At iOffice, we aim to make our word as good as gold, by creating a genuine partnership based on trust. Here is a testimonial from one customer who works for a large healthcare enterprise with a far-flung network.

"As the Director of Facility Operations, responsible for multiple sites and multiple projects, I truly appreciate the manner in which your organization operates and the tools that they provide. The data points listed below are representative of the iOffice team performance that has contributed a strong relationship growing into a synergistic partnership.

- a team of meticulous people searching out ways to improve service
- prompt and courteous responses
- solution oriented rather than service oriented
- best-in-class tools and support for managing space and work orders

"I thank you and your entire team for your contribution to the success of all our projects that you have dedicated time and resources to over the past few years. The tools and the support you provide to make our operational responsibilities more efficient allow for more time to be focused on patient care."

customers. The iOffice portal allows this company to keep its commitments and "stand behind its word." Our software tracks all transactions and allows for real-time reporting and analysis that is transparent to their customers, who can log in at any time to monitor service levels. This creates an atmosphere of trust and commitment between the vendor and its customers. Their word is "as good as gold."

iOFFICE AND THE PROMISE TO DELIVER

Living the "good as gold" code at iOffice means developing customer relationships that begin by listening to customers' needs, then coming up with proposals that reflect those customers, and finally dedicating the proper resources to follow through once we have made a sale. We use some of our own tools to stay organized, communicate with our customers, and meet deadlines. We focus on how to create seamless interfaces with their existing processes and systems. We stick by them through the ups and downs. We have resources in place to answer questions. And we keep our ears tuned for changing needs that trigger this cycle all over again.

Someone can have a lot of enthusiasm and a great attitude about doing a great job, but if they don't have the experience, expertise, skills, capability, and tools, they won't be able to keep their word. The iOffice platform and iOffice people give Facilities Teams the technological tools and support to keep their word and to do a better job.

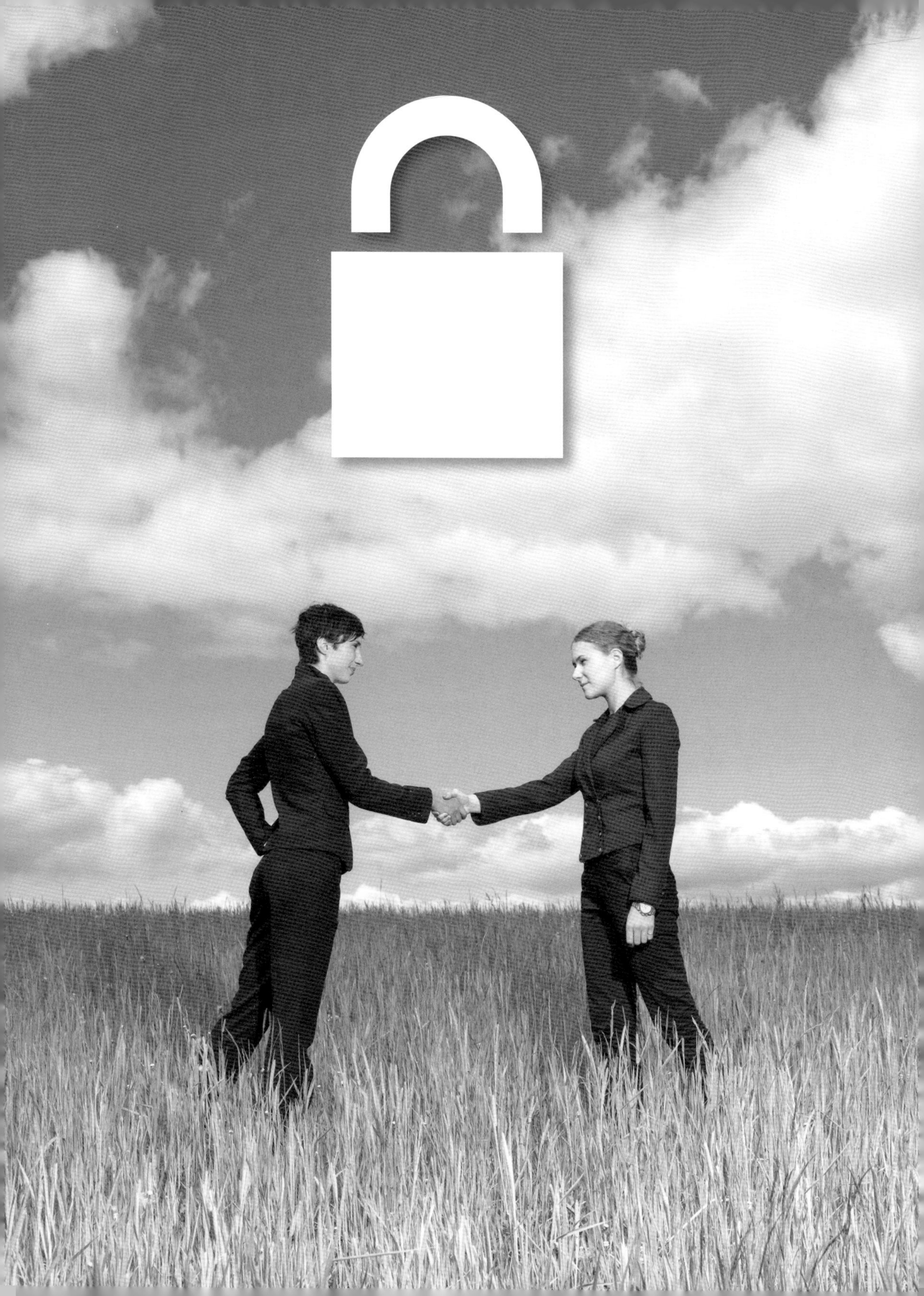

COWBOY HISTORY

CARRIE MARCUS NEIMAN:
STORE FOUNDER AND SALESWOMAN EXTRAORDINAIRE

When Carrie Marcus Neiman opened her first store there, Dallas was a frontier town, but fortunes had already been made. Wealthy women had their clothes custom-made, leaving ready-to-wear for the lower classes. Carrie set out to show these women that this notion was wrong. Using her inimitable sense of the stylish and elegant, Carrie filled her racks with luxurious silks and satins and furs, advancing money to the New York wholesalers who put the clothes together. Within the first month, she had sold out her initial inventory.

Although she worked with partners—her husband, Abraham Neiman, and her brother, Herbert Marcus—it was Carrie's fashion eye that drove the store's success. She was wined and dined in fashion capitals like New York and Paris and Milan, but when she was home, she often spent time waiting on customers and advising them about what to select. Even as Chairman of the Board, she would be seen out on the floor if a favorite customer was in the house.

According to one story, 15 brides had placed orders with Neiman Marcus when, in 1913, the first store—and everything in it—burned to the ground. That disaster did not keep Carrie from keeping her word. The next morning, Carrie rented a room in a nearby hotel, set up shop, and started sewing gowns. All of the weddings were dressed by Neiman Marcus.

Among her charitable activities, Carrie donated 200 garments from her personal closet to form the basis of what is now the Texas Fashion Collection at the University of North Texas in Denton.

Our tools allow the Facilities Manager to keep commitments to the workforce and to deliver services in an efficient, timely manner. As a byproduct, the Facilities Manager can cut costs and create a positive work environment that is beneficial to the workforce, the Executive Team, and the company as a whole. We are committed to making Facilities Managers first-rate Workspace Cowboys, by looking to the future and providing the best-of-breed technology that can help them move from Point A to Point B.

WE ARE COMMITTED TO MAKING FACILITIES MANAGERS FIRST-RATE WORKSPACE COWBOYS, BY LOOKING TO THE FUTURE AND PROVIDING THE BEST-OF-BREED TECHNOLOGY THAT CAN HELP THEM MOVE FROM POINT A TO POINT B.

SHARE

CODE #7: COWBOYS SHARE AROUND THE CAMPFIRE

DURING THE ROUNDUP, cowboys worked together to get a job done. When they gathered around the campfire, they swapped stories and built the personal relationships that sustained the cowboy culture and community. This code will focus on relationship-building and how it supports innovation at the company level and beyond.

When we explored how cowboys keep an eye out for what works, we learned how they took advantage of their diverse origins to adopt tools and methods to get the herd to market. Although the work and roundup formed bonds of one sort, the campfire forged less tangible, but equally important, ties.

As a general rule, cowboys forgot about their differences around the campfire. Through their stories, they shared important information and reinforced the culture that became the cowboy's code. And the circle was an open one. Knowing they might someday find themselves lost and hungry, cowboys always had an extra plate for a stranger passing by.

VOICE OF THE CUSTOMER

THE FUTURE WORKER:
A VIEW FROM A COLLEGE CAMPUS

A Facilities Representative on a university campus shared some perspectives on today's students as a bellwether for tomorrow's workforce. Let's welcome a few students into the campfire circle.

"Students are very tech savvy. They're very mobile. They all have iPhones or Androids or iPads. The Y Generation has short attention spans, and they expect immediate gratification. We have to adapt to that. We have to keep up with what is going to be the best new thing, because students have high expectations for service levels.

"Mobility is a huge component of it. Think how far things have advanced in the last five years. The iPad didn't even exist five years ago. Now everybody has a tablet. A tablet was a Panasonic Toughbook five years ago. It weighed eight pounds and was two inches thick. So things have changed dramatically, and we don't see that slowing down anytime in the near future.

"We've all become dependent on our mobile devices. We're used to instant access to information and instant access to updates. If Diego Perez is expecting a package from Amazon, he'll sign up for email alerts from UPS. He'll know when his package has arrived, sometimes before the mail center knows. He'll come to the mail room and say, 'Hey, my new iPhone is here. It just got delivered five minutes ago. Where is it?' Diego doesn't care that the loading dock is upstairs, receiving 400 packages a day and needing to get them downstairs and on the shelves. His iPhone is here. He wants it right now.

"At the same time, Diego may not know where the stamp goes on an envelope. We had a big challenge with students throwing away very confidential documents, such as bank statements and credit card offers. They would just pull mail out of their mailbox and toss it right into the open recycle bin. Bank statements and credit card offers have all kinds of PII (personally identifiable information) that puts the students at risk for identity theft. Our manager would dig through the recycle bins, pull out sensitive material, and take it over to the shred bin.

"We're trying to go above and beyond to educate students who don't have any real-world experience. They don't know what identity theft is. They see the envelope and think, 'I can look at this on-line, so I'll just toss this in the trash.' They don't understand how risky that can be. We now have shredding kiosks that are painted with the school logo and the school colors. This shredder with a video screen runs advertising and movie trailers. Now the kids bring in boxes of stuff from their dorms and shred it themselves, watching the video.

"Another component is social media. Social media isn't going to go away anytime soon—just the opposite. It's definitely a part of that younger generation's culture. The reality is that if kids don't have it, they can't do what they need to do. They use it for school and academics. They use it for clubs. They use it to manage their lives.

"How do we integrate social media into our business operations? Whatever the latest, greatest social media trend is (whether it's Foursquare, Facebook, or Twitter), we probably need to be aware of it and consider integrating and using those tools ourselves. For example, can we feed information into Twitter, so Diego can see what the package wait time is? Can we use social media to market ourselves and our services? Can we notify Diego when a conveyor is down or some UPS packages are delayed because of a storm?

"Every university is competing for the same pool of high school seniors. And while nobody's going to make a decision about where to go to college based on the mail services or on the copy centers at the university, it does play into the overall impression when students come for a campus tour. 'Is this a high-tech, fun place? Or is this a stodgy, old-fashioned school?' they'll ask themselves.

"Eventually this will translate to the workforce—'Do I want to work at Google, or do I want to work at this old, stodgy law firm?' Companies can't continue to manage their services in the same old way if they are expecting to attract talent that's under 30. Young people want a new, advanced way of working. They're going to look down on an organization where they have to fill out a paper form to have a copy printed, or they don't know where their mail is, or they have to sit in the same workspace every day with walls closed off. What happens today in the student world is going to happen in the corporate world five years from now.

"Many companies still say, 'We're going to have private offices and private workstations. We believe that people need quiet workspace.' But the talent pool is demanding new work environments. They want to engage in a different way. College students will bring a new mentality and thought process to the workplace, replacing us old guys. It's going to happen. At the university, we're getting to practice on tomorrow's workforce that will someday be made up of Millennials or the Generation Y population."

WIDE OPEN WORKSPACE

THE CAMPFIRE IN THE WORKSPACE ARENA

Workspace Cowboys recognize that one cowboy doesn't have all the answers. In fact, diversity leads to greatness. Texas is a hotbed of diversity. Texas is a state with less regulation than most, a state that is open to different cultures, a state that focuses on what works.

We at iOffice believe that a "wide open mind" is essential for the innovation that is needed for a Wide Open Workspace. Productivity goes up when you share your knowledge freely (like the cowboys around the campfire). If people are shut off from others, afraid to show any weakness, they will miss out on the opportunities and fun that result when different perspectives find a common ground. When people share ideas, talk about where they are, or ask for help when they need it, productivity, innovation, and effectiveness are raised to a whole new level.

WORKSPACE COWBOYS RECOGNIZE THAT ONE COWBOY DOESN'T HAVE ALL THE ANSWERS. IN FACT, DIVERSITY LEADS TO GREATNESS. TEXAS IS A HOTBED OF DIVERSITY. TEXAS IS A STATE WITH LESS REGULATION THAN MOST, A STATE THAT IS OPEN TO DIFFERENT CULTURES, A STATE THAT FOCUSES ON WHAT WORKS.

The campfire ambiance in the workplace comes from many small collaborations and from the rapport that is built with social interaction that is *not* connected to getting a task done. Google and Yahoo! create casual places to get their employees socializing with one another. These

CONTEMPORARY BIZ

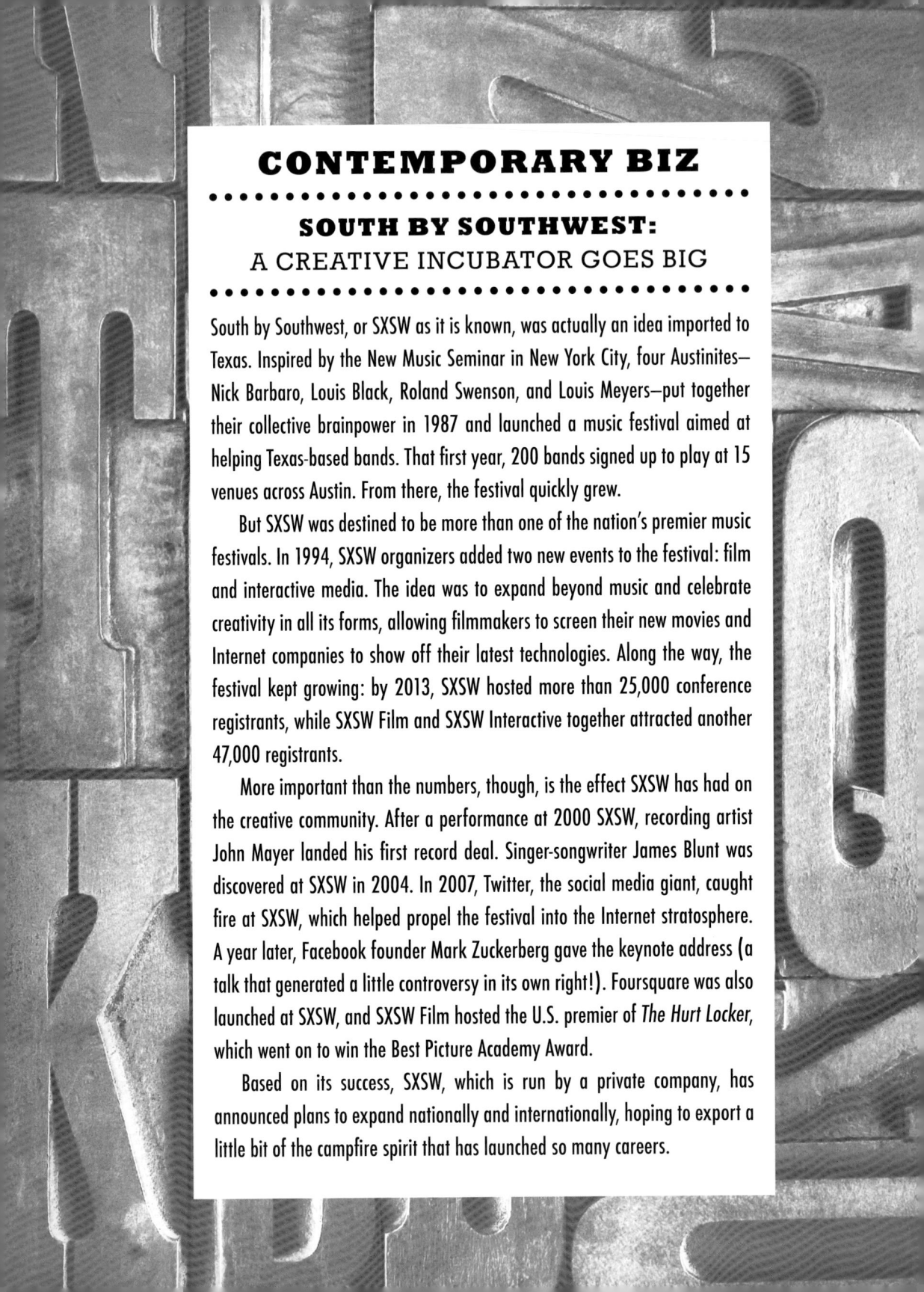

SOUTH BY SOUTHWEST:
A CREATIVE INCUBATOR GOES BIG

South by Southwest, or SXSW as it is known, was actually an idea imported to Texas. Inspired by the New Music Seminar in New York City, four Austinites—Nick Barbaro, Louis Black, Roland Swenson, and Louis Meyers—put together their collective brainpower in 1987 and launched a music festival aimed at helping Texas-based bands. That first year, 200 bands signed up to play at 15 venues across Austin. From there, the festival quickly grew.

But SXSW was destined to be more than one of the nation's premier music festivals. In 1994, SXSW organizers added two new events to the festival: film and interactive media. The idea was to expand beyond music and celebrate creativity in all its forms, allowing filmmakers to screen their new movies and Internet companies to show off their latest technologies. Along the way, the festival kept growing: by 2013, SXSW hosted more than 25,000 conference registrants, while SXSW Film and SXSW Interactive together attracted another 47,000 registrants.

More important than the numbers, though, is the effect SXSW has had on the creative community. After a performance at 2000 SXSW, recording artist John Mayer landed his first record deal. Singer-songwriter James Blunt was discovered at SXSW in 2004. In 2007, Twitter, the social media giant, caught fire at SXSW, which helped propel the festival into the Internet stratosphere. A year later, Facebook founder Mark Zuckerberg gave the keynote address (a talk that generated a little controversy in its own right!). Foursquare was also launched at SXSW, and SXSW Film hosted the U.S. premier of *The Hurt Locker*, which went on to win the Best Picture Academy Award.

Based on its success, SXSW, which is run by a private company, has announced plans to expand nationally and internationally, hoping to export a little bit of the campfire spirit that has launched so many careers.

companies hope that personal camaraderie will lead to creativity and innovation.

When discussing trailblazing (Code #1), we mentioned how Sabre Holdings, a company that serves the travel industry, introduced Flexspace. As part of that initiative, Sabre has created workspaces for different communities. When you arrive at the company, you roll your file cabinet to whatever community you want to work in that day. Diverse connections are formed, as needed, to respond to company challenges.

The campfire principle extends beyond a specific enterprise. In many arenas, the age of competition has been replaced by an age of strategic alliances. More and more companies see an advantage in brainstorming together to resolve problems and enhance innovation. Developments like the cloud and tools for sharing, like Dropbox, permit people to gather around a virtual campfire, even though they may be separated by many miles.

ONE CAMPFIRE INNOVATION THAT SPREAD

We want to share an example from our experience, where three parties came together to develop an innovation that has since spread within the sector of higher education.

Not long ago, a major university with 15,000 students and 30,000 employees faced a major problem in delivering student mail. Although mailed letters are almost a thing of the past, mailed packages are booming due to purchases over the Internet. Poor service at the mail center was a point of

COWBOY HISTORY

DANIEL WEBSTER WALLACE:
OPENING NEW FRONTIERS FOR BLACK RANCHERS

At first glance, Daniel Webster Wallace wasn't a typical cowboy. Born to slaves near Inez, just before the Civil War broke out, he grew up working the cotton fields in Flatonia, Texas, dreaming of the trail.

But in the important ways, Wallace was exactly what you'd expect from a cowboy. In 1877, freed from slavery and fed up with the crushing labor of the cotton field, he joined a cattle drive and found his passion. Over the next eight years, Wallace drove cattle and wrangled horses for some of the most respected names in the industry. When he wasn't riding, he was working to improve himself. Lacking a formal education, Wallace enrolled himself in the second grade at age 25 and learned to read and write.

Throughout these years, a new dream took hold in Wallace's fertile imagination: not content to herd other men's cattle, Wallace wanted to be a rancher himself.

Given the time and place, the odds of an African-American son of slaves owning a successful cattle ranch in Texas were astronomically thin. But Wallace's energy and character had earned him lasting friendships, especially with one Clay Mann.

Wallace was working on Mann's ranch, branding his cattle and driving them to market, when the two men worked out a plan. At the time, Wallace's monthly salary was $30. He took only $5 each month, and Mann saved the rest for him, slowly building up a nest egg Wallace could use to make his dream a reality. In 1885, Wallace bought 1,280 acres southeast of Loraine. In 1891—two years after his friend Mann passed away—Wallace moved his own cattle onto his own land and struck out to make his own way.

The cattle business back then wasn't easy, but it didn't take too long for Wallace to make a name for himself. He even became a respected member of the Texas and Southwestern Cattle Raisers Association, and when he died in 1939, he had an accumulated personal wealth of more than $1 million.

By being a first-rate cattleman, Wallace paved the way for other African Americans to join the campfire. He was buried on his ranch.

dissatisfaction with the students. No proactive notification of packages, a 30-minute wait in a long line, and lost packages were constant complaints from digitally savvy kids.

One of our customers that provides business services asked us to partner with them to prepare a bid in response to the competitive request for proposals opened by the university. By offering a solution to satisfy student expectations, we won the job. The iOffice Mail Module was tailored specifically for the university environment. When a package arrives at the mail center, it is checked into the software. Automatically, the student is notified by email. At the mail center, the student scans his or her I.D. at a computer kiosk, like the ones at the airport. That triggers a process to search for and pick up the package. The kiosk directs the student to the window and signature pad. In about two minutes, the transaction is closed and recorded.

THE iOFFICE MAIL MODULE WAS TAILORED SPECIFICALLY FOR THE UNIVERSITY ENVIRONMENT.

Students like being notified via their mobile devices, and they like retrieving their packages immediately. The system generates reports for the university administration about mail volume and delivery performance. This helps the institution ensure that is has an up-to-date service that can help to attract students to the campus. Since being introduced, this application has been adopted by more than a half dozen other university campuses. Word spreads around the campfire.

iOFFICE AND THE CAMPFIRE

Continuous improvement is a philosophy embraced by many market leaders. At iOffice, we try to instill the mindset of constant innovation in our staff and in our customer relationships.

With respect to our staff, we have aimed to attract diverse talent who work as a team. We welcome dogs in the office; they create a homier atmosphere that promotes bonding. Working companions to the cowboys, dogs definitely belong around the campfire!

We also try to create the sense of campfire with our customers. Experienced resources support them during sales, implementation, and ongoing management. We aim for a high level of service and constantly roll out new features to make our products work better. Needs keep changing. A best-of-breed technology must stay ahead of the curve. Staying at the forefront is possible when customers trust you with their problems and ride with you to blaze new trails.

Innovation and excellence come when players with different skills tackle a common problem. Collaboration is embedded in many of the other cowboy codes. Trailblazing, finding what works, keeping your word, getting together for the roundup—all of these create a positive, reinforcing circle that stimulates innovation, which in turn strengthens further teamwork and collaboration.

Below, we will recap some iOffice innovations that resulted from Workspace Cowboys sharing around the campfire. For each innovation, iOffice worked with the Workspace Cowboys of its customers. Once developed, these innovations enhanced our offerings to other companies, thus pushing the discipline of workspace management forward. The multiple innovations emerging from the same customer relationship demonstrate the "virtuous circle" at work.

- With a software company, we developed a mobile application that allows users to search for and reserve space. It also allows for tracking of real-time use of space.
- With a healthcare network, we adapted the Space Management Module to provide a user-friendly, cost-effective tool for smaller clinics.
- Also for that network, we developed a mobile application for site inspections, using the smartphone.
- Currently, with the same customer, we are testing OpenSpace (the application to manage flexspace) in a healthcare environment.
- With our imaging and print solutions customer, we tested and expanded the software as a service (SaaS) solution, taking full advantage of cloud capabilities.
- Partnering with that same company, we developed the kiosk-based package notification and tracking application for students, engaging closely with the Project Manager of the university.
- Also for this company in the imaging and print solutions industry, we devised a solution for managed document services (MDS) that allows for automatic capture of data from printers and copiers.

WIDE OPEN WORKSPACE

We are working to extend the reach of the campfire, to encompass a larger group of Workspace Cowboys.

- We created a web-based "Idea Community" for customers to share ideas about features and functionality to enhance our platform.

- We publish the iOffice blog to share software tips, success stories, and other information that can help customers and other companies.

- We collaborate with firms with different expertises to provide more value to customers, including Rackspace, Balderdash, and FotoNotes.

- We are planning a customer forum for in-person sharing and networking.

- We are sharing experiences and success stories through the publication of this book.

CONTEMPORARY BIZ

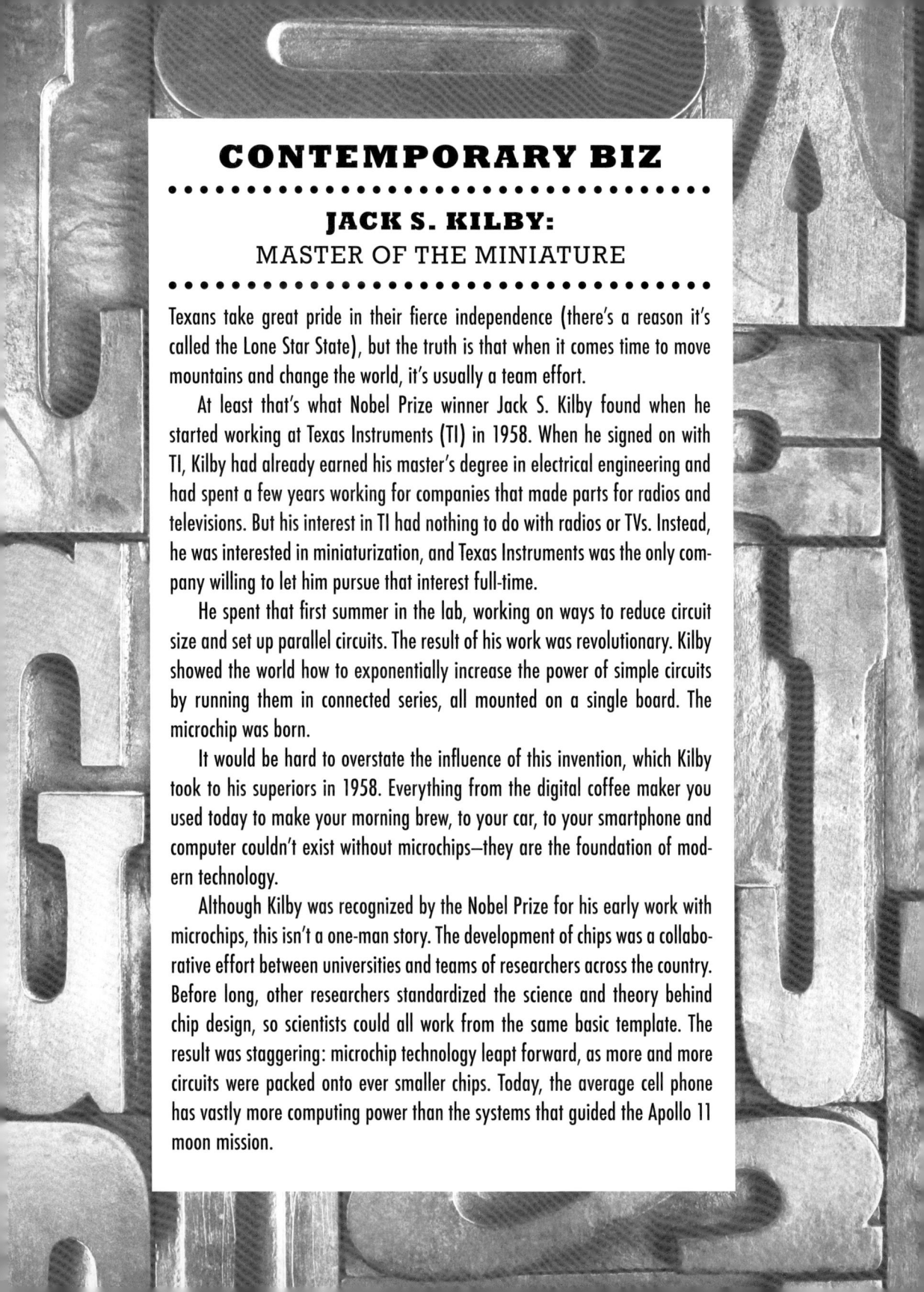

JACK S. KILBY:
MASTER OF THE MINIATURE

Texans take great pride in their fierce independence (there's a reason it's called the Lone Star State), but the truth is that when it comes time to move mountains and change the world, it's usually a team effort.

At least that's what Nobel Prize winner Jack S. Kilby found when he started working at Texas Instruments (TI) in 1958. When he signed on with TI, Kilby had already earned his master's degree in electrical engineering and had spent a few years working for companies that made parts for radios and televisions. But his interest in TI had nothing to do with radios or TVs. Instead, he was interested in miniaturization, and Texas Instruments was the only company willing to let him pursue that interest full-time.

He spent that first summer in the lab, working on ways to reduce circuit size and set up parallel circuits. The result of his work was revolutionary. Kilby showed the world how to exponentially increase the power of simple circuits by running them in connected series, all mounted on a single board. The microchip was born.

It would be hard to overstate the influence of this invention, which Kilby took to his superiors in 1958. Everything from the digital coffee maker you used today to make your morning brew, to your car, to your smartphone and computer couldn't exist without microchips—they are the foundation of modern technology.

Although Kilby was recognized by the Nobel Prize for his early work with microchips, this isn't a one-man story. The development of chips was a collaborative effort between universities and teams of researchers across the country. Before long, other researchers standardized the science and theory behind chip design, so scientists could all work from the same basic template. The result was staggering: microchip technology leapt forward, as more and more circuits were packed onto ever smaller chips. Today, the average cell phone has vastly more computing power than the systems that guided the Apollo 11 moon mission.

LOYAL

CODE #8: COWBOYS RIDE FOR THE BRAND

COWBOYS HAD A code of honor. Although they may have moved from ranch to ranch, they felt a strong bond to the brand they were working for. Even though the man who owned the herd often wasn't there to supervise the roundup or the cattle drive, the cowboys could be trusted to ride for his brand. Cowboys were also part of a special "club" with its own code of ethics that included values like honesty, taking care of others, and reinforcing the code itself.

"Riding for the brand" is about commitment and loyalty to something bigger than oneself. Riding for the brand is evidenced in sports jerseys and college sweatshirts and company logos on our shoes. In the business context, you might ride for your company or your profession. At iOffice, we believe riding for the brand means championing workspace as a transformative force. That is how we see our commitment to the Wide Open Workspace movement.

VOICE OF THE CUSTOMER

LEVERAGING TECHNOLOGY FOR LEADERSHIP

Armed with the right technology, Facilities Managers can lead the way as their companies ride into the Wide Open Workspace.

STRATEGIC SPACE UTILIZATION. "Leveraging technology such as the iOffice tool is certainly going to determine the level of success leaders have in managing space real-time. The ability to project space needs, manage reservations for mobile workers, and provide ease of access to view various spaces across an organization will play a big role going forward in how well space utilization strategies develop. The more information available for users and the more Data Managers can use to understand utilization, the better the strategies can be developed and executed."

A POSITION OF LEADERSHIP. "In this company, leaders at the highest levels of the organization are setting the tone to drive many of the workplace changes taking place today. As a whole, the organization realizes that in order to retain and continue to build a growing team of talented individuals, the workplace must evolve. Real estate is a critical component in any organization where large volumes of space are needed for offices and distribution; however, today there are opportunities for facilities management to take a larger and more impactful role. If a Facilities Management Team positions itself correctly with the right technology, they will become an indispensable piece of the corporate structure. Their leadership can drive efficiencies in space management, asset management, capital preservation, corporate citizenship, minimizing downtime of critical systems—the list goes on and on."

RIDING FOR THE BRAND IN THE 21ST CENTURY

Texas entrepreneurs have a history of riding for the community brand, investing in the various communities they serve. For example, in a 2013 survey by Thumbtack of the friendliest cities for small businesses in the United States, four Texas cities fell in the top ten: Austin, San Antonio, Houston, and Dallas. The state's commitment to business creates a climate for networking, hiring, and licensing. This yields not just population growth, but also loyalty.

You can usually spot a company that generates loyalty and commitment in its constituents, both workers and employees. People speak with pride and a sense of belonging. Southwest Airlines is such a company. Whole Foods Market is another. People who work at Whole Foods really value what the company stands for. Even Whole Foods' customers understand its mission and feel a part of it.

Of course, not all companies enjoy that kind of loyalty or alignment. Downsizing and layoffs separate workers from their brand. In the knowledge economy, companies are wide open. The power structure is much less vertical; many levels of supervision have disappeared. Job opportunities allow workers to move from one company to another. Pay and benefits have less power to retain talent than once thought. Younger people, including many Millennials, want to feel that they're part of something bigger. Furthermore, a direct correlation exists between employee loyalty and customer loyalty, so riding for the brand is not just "nice to have" but a competitive imperative.

WORKSPACE COWBOYS RIDE FOR THE BRAND

No matter what their titles may be (Real Estate, Facilities, or Workplace Manager), Workspace Cowboys need to ride for their company brand by constantly asking the right questions: "Are we managing our business in a way that is beneficial for the customer?" "Are we taking care of our employees?" "Are we investing in the right tools?" With the transformation of the workspace, the Workspace Cowboy has a critical role in attracting the right cows to the herd and encouraging them to stay.

First-rate Workspace Cowboys really understand their organization and how their people work. They create an environment and a workspace that represents their brand—that is uniquely based on their company and their industry. Perhaps that space looks like Google, freewheeling and without fixed desks. Perhaps it looks like an energy company, where the geoscientists and geologists need big work tables and private workspaces.

THE SABRE HOLDINGS CASE—RIDING FOR THE BRAND AND RAISING THE BAR

In 2012, Sabre Holdings published a detailed case study about their move to Flexspace. It is recommended reading for anyone who wants to understand the impact workspace can have on business performance.

The Workspace Cowboys at Sabre pushed the frontiers at their company and in the profession. Let's see how Sabre's Facilities Team raised the bar for all Workspace Cowboys.

CONTEMPORARY BIZ

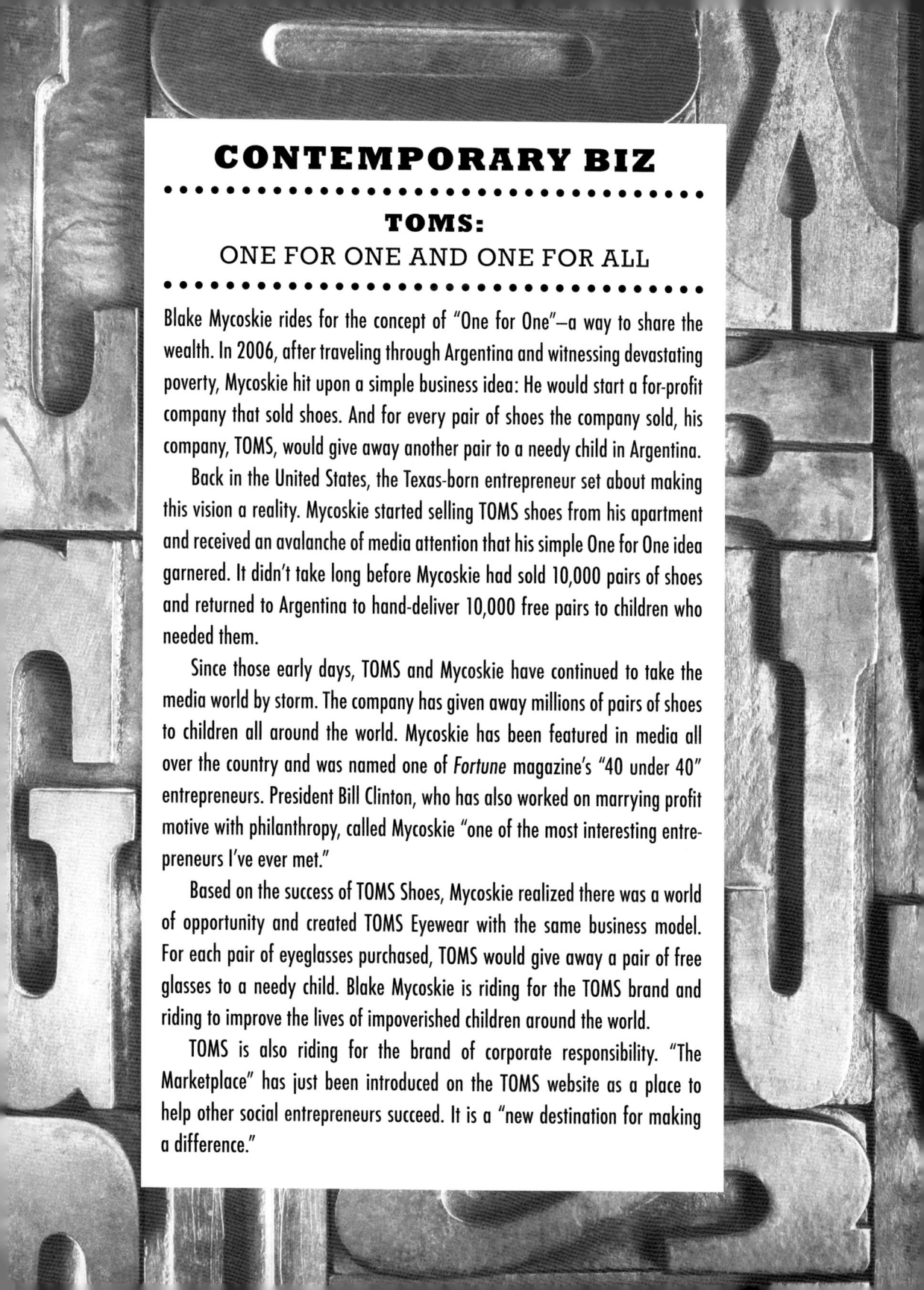

TOMS:
ONE FOR ONE AND ONE FOR ALL

Blake Mycoskie rides for the concept of "One for One"—a way to share the wealth. In 2006, after traveling through Argentina and witnessing devastating poverty, Mycoskie hit upon a simple business idea: He would start a for-profit company that sold shoes. And for every pair of shoes the company sold, his company, TOMS, would give away another pair to a needy child in Argentina.

Back in the United States, the Texas-born entrepreneur set about making this vision a reality. Mycoskie started selling TOMS shoes from his apartment and received an avalanche of media attention that his simple One for One idea garnered. It didn't take long before Mycoskie had sold 10,000 pairs of shoes and returned to Argentina to hand-deliver 10,000 free pairs to children who needed them.

Since those early days, TOMS and Mycoskie have continued to take the media world by storm. The company has given away millions of pairs of shoes to children all around the world. Mycoskie has been featured in media all over the country and was named one of *Fortune* magazine's "40 under 40" entrepreneurs. President Bill Clinton, who has also worked on marrying profit motive with philanthropy, called Mycoskie "one of the most interesting entrepreneurs I've ever met."

Based on the success of TOMS Shoes, Mycoskie realized there was a world of opportunity and created TOMS Eyewear with the same business model. For each pair of eyeglasses purchased, TOMS would give away a pair of free glasses to a needy child. Blake Mycoskie is riding for the TOMS brand and riding to improve the lives of impoverished children around the world.

TOMS is also riding for the brand of corporate responsibility. "The Marketplace" has just been introduced on the TOMS website as a place to help other social entrepreneurs succeed. It is a "new destination for making a difference."

COWBOY HISTORY

STEPHEN AUSTIN:
RIDING FOR TEXAS

When Stephen Austin arrived in San Antonio in 1821, he had no idea he would spend the rest of his life fighting to establish the world-famous brand that would become the State of Texas.

Austin was in Texas, not—as we mentioned earlier—because of his own dream, but because of a promise he had made to his father to help settle 300 families in the rugged territory. Although there were plenty of willing colonists ready to gamble on the dusty, Mexican-controlled patch of land after the Panic of 1819, Austin's plans ran into immediate trouble. Newly independent from Spain, the Mexican government announced that it would no longer honor the original land grant agreement with Moses Austin. So, Stephen had to travel to Mexico City to try to broker a new agreement.

The negotiations went back and forth for years. Austin was a persistent and conservative advocate for the colonists, whose numbers grew steadily as he received more contracts to bring people in.

As such things often go, however, tensions arose between the growing colonies and the faraway Mexican administrative government, which never had much interest in policing the colonies. There was the question of control over the burgeoning territories; in most cases, the colonists, who numbered 8,000 by 1832, were sympathetic to the United States. The U.S. had a strong interest in buying the territory that Mexico was none too eager to give up. There was the issue of continued immigration, which Mexico banned in 1830. And there was the question of slavery, which was unsettled because many of the new colonists brought slaves with them, even though slavery had been abolished in Mexico.

Austin himself was a cautious politician. As more voices called for a separate state constitution, he pushed for slower measures and deeper engagement with the Mexican government. But when the tide turned, Austin put the colonists' views ahead of his own and traveled again to Mexico City to lobby for a Texas state government. He didn't make it home right away: Mexican President Santa Anna had Austin arrested for insurrection and jailed, even though no charges were ever brought against him and no court had jurisdiction over his case.

By the time he was released in 1835, Austin returned to a territory ready to shake off its allegiance to Mexico. Even though he still had misgivings, when Texans called for a convention, Austin lent his support to becoming part of the United States. The election of delegates proceeded, followed by war. Austin commanded volunteer troops against the Mexican Army at San Antonio. At the same time, he worked to convince the United States to support the Texas territory and agree to annex the state when it declared its independence from Mexico.

By the time he died at age 43, Austin had done more to establish the State of Texas than anyone else. He did this by being loyal to Texas first and foremost, even when the views of the Texans themselves were at odds with his own careful nature.

"The prosperity of Texas has been the object of my labors," he wrote in 1836, "the idol of my existence." Austin was truly a man who rode for the brand.

At first glance, the Sabre Holdings case is about embedding flexible space in a company where many of the employees do not travel extensively. However, the program went far beyond reshaping facilities to transforming the way business is done. In most companies, Facilities Managers strive to support the business strategy; at Sabre, planning and executing the Flexspace program was an integral component and even a driver of the business strategy. Sabre's Corporate Real Estate Managers are full strategic partners, helping to shape the possibilities for the future. Thus, **being a strategic partner** is the first "bar" for today's Workspace Cowboys.

AT iOFFICE, WE BELIEVE RIDING FOR THE BRAND MEANS CHAMPIONING WORKSPACE AS A TRANSFORMATIVE FORCE. THAT IS HOW WE SEE OUR COMMITMENT TO THE WIDE OPEN WORKSPACE MOVEMENT.

The Flexspace program was not implemented in a vacuum, as a standalone initiative. Rather, it complemented and was able to leverage numerous other corporate investments, including

- one of the first LEED-certified headquarters in the United States with flexible, open architecture and enabling technology;
- a VoIP (Voice-over-Internet-Protocol) telephone system; and
- mobile laptops to replace stationary desktop computers.

Such decisions do not rest on guesswork or the whim of a single area; rather, diverse professionals, including the Facilities experts, identified future trends and built a strong strategic business case. Thus, we add another bar for the Workspace Cowboy—**a long-term vision and an analytical mindset.**

NO MATTER WHAT THEIR TITLES MAY BE (REAL ESTATE, FACILITIES, OR WORKPLACE MANAGER), WORKSPACE COWBOYS NEED TO RIDE FOR THEIR COMPANY BRAND BY CONSTANTLY ASKING THE RIGHT QUESTIONS: "ARE WE MANAGING OUR BUSINESS IN A WAY THAT IS BENEFICIAL FOR THE CUSTOMER?" "ARE WE TAKING CARE OF OUR EMPLOYEES?" "ARE WE INVESTING IN THE RIGHT TOOLS?"

Speaking of analysis, most companies have some type of "balanced scorecard" or other tool to measure performance. For real estate, traditional measures are square foot per employee or real estate cost per employee. Sabre's VP of Corporate Real Estate realized that a different metric was needed—one that would measure utilization of space. You've no doubt heard the expression, "We are what we measure." Correctly **defining and measuring performance** for the Facilities function is another challenge for the Workspace Cowboy.

Measurement brings the idea of benchmarking to mind, that is, looking outside of your company and industry for best practices. The Sabre team studied well-tested approaches, including "hoteling" (used by service firms with a traveling workforce) and transformable spaces (common

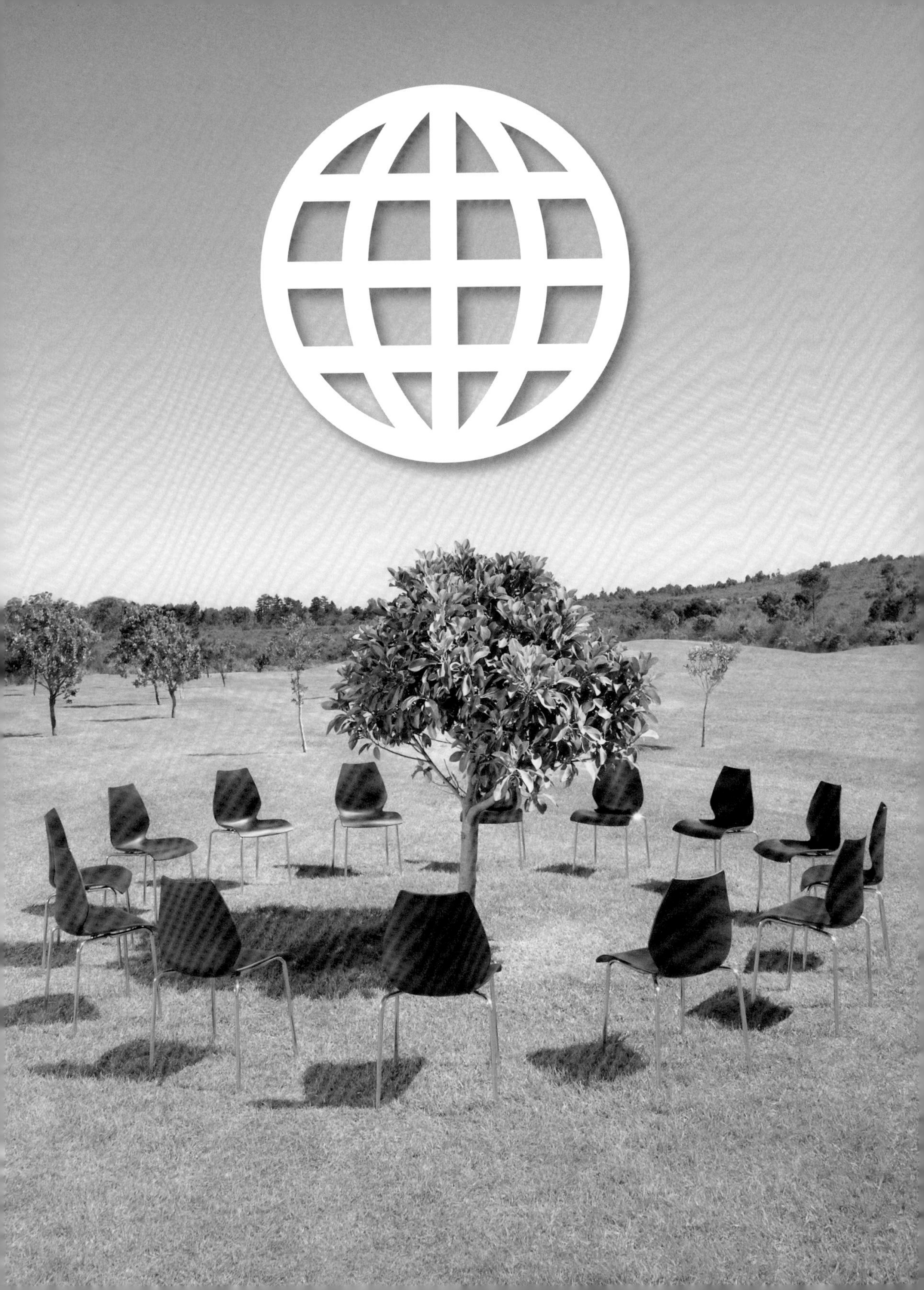

in fast-growing start-ups that prize collaboration). Sabre also engaged external partners who brought experiences to complement their own. Successful Workspace Cowboys **find a balance between "what works" and what must be customized.**

Real estate represents a major component of a company's cost structure, typically the second largest after human resource costs. As such, it is usually a target when companies want to trim operating expenses. Seeking ways to improve the performance of the people and assets, most Facilities Managers identify important but incremental adjustments.

SUCCESSFUL WORKSPACE COWBOYS FIND A BALANCE BETWEEN "WHAT WORKS" AND WHAT MUST BE CUSTOMIZED.

Flexspace at Sabre was anything but incremental. It was a dramatic break with the past, with dramatic results—the program cut the corporate real estate footprint in half! Sabre embraced radical new ways of doing things that were a "step function" down in costs—a reduction of "annual operational expenses by $10 million within three years." Workspace Cowboys **think big!**

The transition to flexspace at Sabre and other companies can be a daunting challenge. Sabre brought a change management professional on to their team to orchestrate the complex process within a very aggressive timeframe. The case study explains how the human dynamics were managed with meticulous detail. Factors like CEO leadership, multifaceted communication, and manager/employee

CONTEMPORARY BIZ

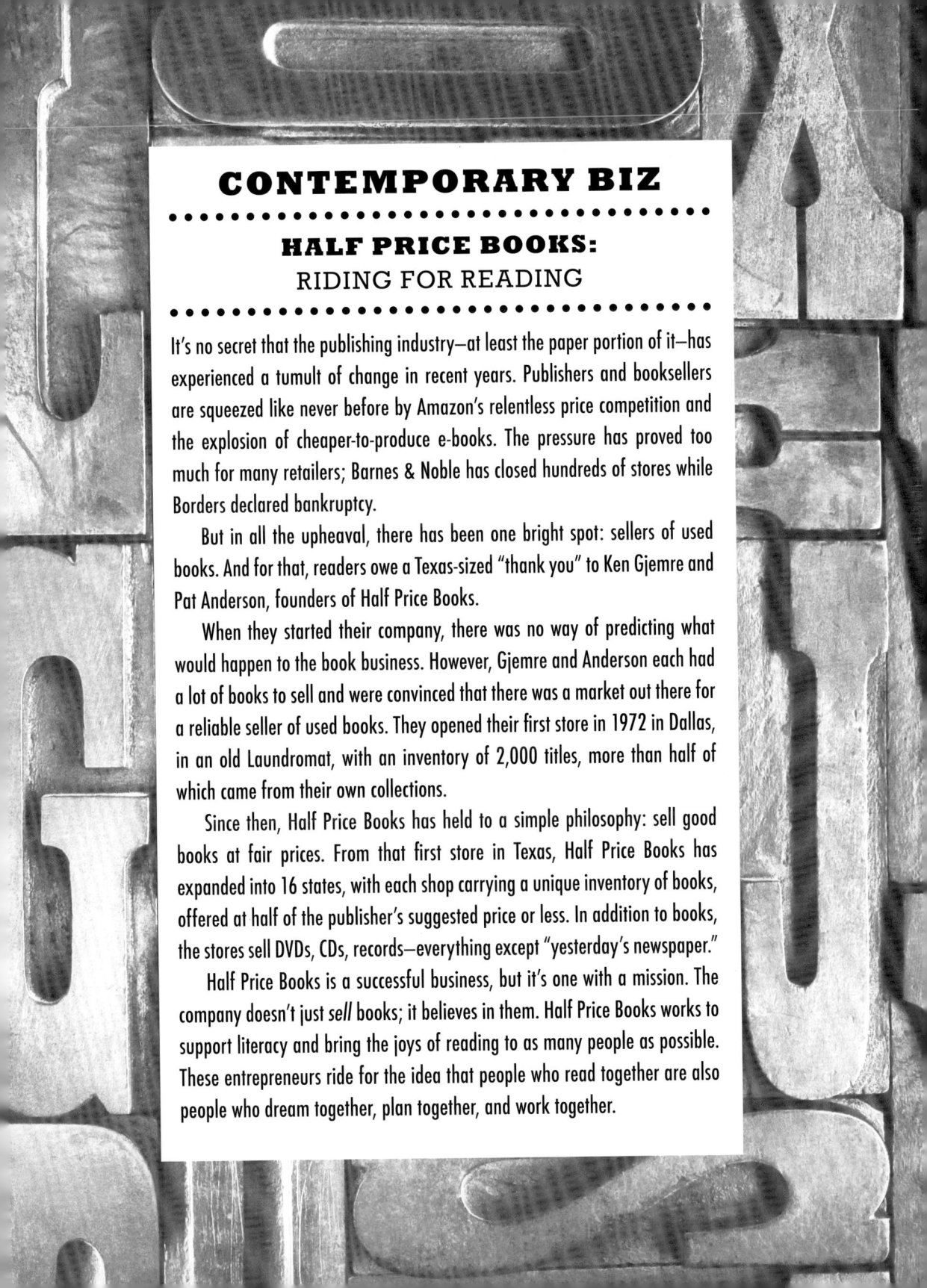

HALF PRICE BOOKS:
RIDING FOR READING

It's no secret that the publishing industry—at least the paper portion of it—has experienced a tumult of change in recent years. Publishers and booksellers are squeezed like never before by Amazon's relentless price competition and the explosion of cheaper-to-produce e-books. The pressure has proved too much for many retailers; Barnes & Noble has closed hundreds of stores while Borders declared bankruptcy.

But in all the upheaval, there has been one bright spot: sellers of used books. And for that, readers owe a Texas-sized "thank you" to Ken Gjemre and Pat Anderson, founders of Half Price Books.

When they started their company, there was no way of predicting what would happen to the book business. However, Gjemre and Anderson each had a lot of books to sell and were convinced that there was a market out there for a reliable seller of used books. They opened their first store in 1972 in Dallas, in an old Laundromat, with an inventory of 2,000 titles, more than half of which came from their own collections.

Since then, Half Price Books has held to a simple philosophy: sell good books at fair prices. From that first store in Texas, Half Price Books has expanded into 16 states, with each shop carrying a unique inventory of books, offered at half of the publisher's suggested price or less. In addition to books, the stores sell DVDs, CDs, records—everything except "yesterday's newspaper."

Half Price Books is a successful business, but it's one with a mission. The company doesn't just *sell* books; it believes in them. Half Price Books works to support literacy and bring the joys of reading to as many people as possible. These entrepreneurs ride for the idea that people who read together are also people who dream together, plan together, and work together.

participation were all critical to the successful transition. "Never underestimate the human element," warns the case. Thus, **careful change management** is another skill needed by today's Workspace Cowboy.

The term *Flexspace* was coined by Sabre for its flexible workspace program. Like *Kleenex*, a word that started as a brand name, it has become generic. Giving the program an identity and sharing "challenges and best practices with Corporate Real Estate and Sustainability professionals" are two ways that Sabre spearheaded a professional movement—*flexspace*. **Adding value to the profession** as a whole is another bar for those who wish to "ride for the brand."

Sabre is not the only company that is leading the way; however, it is one of few that have documented their experience so thoroughly. Sabre's story covers a decade of innovation and transformation from which others can learn. Let's recap some of the bars that Sabre's Facilities Team raised for other Workspace Cowboys:

- being a strategic partner with the business
- having a long-term vision and an analytical mindset
- inventing new metrics
- balancing "what works" with what must be customized
- thinking big!
- managing change carefully
- adding value to other professionals and companies

That's a tall order. Are you up for the challenge?

iOFFICE AND RIDING FOR THE BRAND

iOffice rides for our brand. We ride for the Wide Open Workspace by being committed to our customers' success. Customer success means delivering technology that works as promised. Customer success is providing the correct resources to implement solutions successfully within our customers' environments. Customer success is staying abreast of the marketplace and technology trends so that we provide "continuous improvement" in our solutions. Customer success is leading our customers on their own journey into the Wide Open Workspace.

INSIGHT

NEW FRONTIERS AWAIT

IT IS AN EXCITING TIME to be in the world of facilities management. We hope these cowboy codes have provided inspiration and insight into the challenges of this changing frontier. Even as we reflect on Texas history, we are bullish on the future of the state and we are watching for hints of what might lie around the next bend to influence the facilities profession.

One trend is the way in which business schools are dealing with space. For decades, students being groomed as "captains of industry" in Masters of Business Administration (MBA) programs sat in the same seat for the entire year, in an amphitheater where the only parts that moved were the blackboard and the professor. Recently, Harvard Business School retooled a building on its campus to create classrooms with mobile desks and chairs, to facilitate small group and team discussions. If MBA students experience the benefits of flexible quarters from the first day of class, they are more likely to understand the power of space configurations when they hold leadership positions.

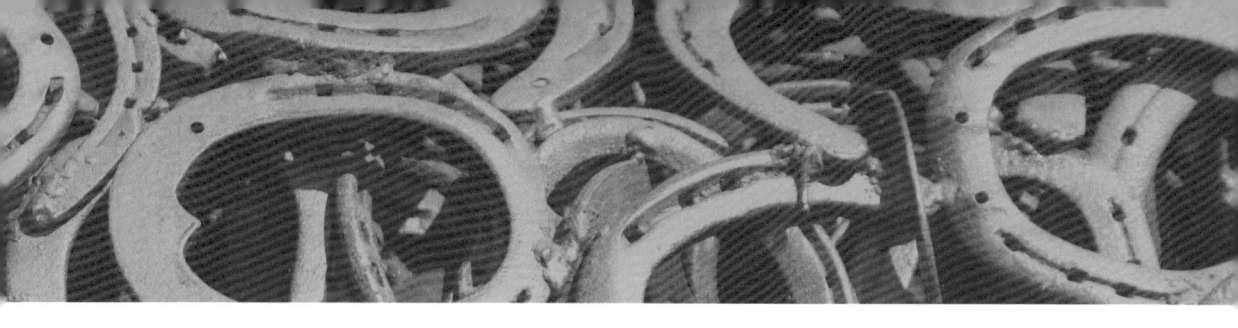

COWBOY HISTORY

TEXAS:
THE FUTURE OF AMERICA?

Throughout this book, we have looked back at Texas history for inspiration. However, the State of Texas also provides some clues about what may lie ahead. In October 2013, *Time* magazine's cover story was "The United States of Texas: Why the Lone Star State Is America's Future." Economist and libertarian Tyler Cowen describes how trends in Texas suggest forces that will shape the United States as a whole in the decades to come.

Cowen writes, "Texas is America's fastest-growing large state, with three of the top five fastest-growing cities in the country: Austin, Dallas and Houston. . . . Since 2000, 1 million more people have moved to Texas from other states than have left."

He goes on to explain why so many people are moving to the Lone Star State. "Americans are seeking out a cheaper cost of living and a less regulated climate in which to do business; Texas has that in spades. And did we mention there's no state income tax?"

In addition to the cost of living, lower taxes, and less regulation, Cowen cites job growth and the rise of the "new cowboys"—people seeking a simpler way of life rather than big success.

Cowen cites a bumper sticker that reads, "I wasn't born in Texas, but I got here as fast as I could." He portrays Texas as a place where people can make a fresh start. Just like the cowboys of another era, people find new opportunities in the wide open spaces of Texas.

One person who is bullish on the state and its future is the Chancellor of the University of Texas System, Francisco G. Cigarroa, who brings his multicultural, multidisciplinary vision to the 15 institutions that make up the university system. The graduates of UT will be among those who shape the big ranch that is the State of Texas, with an impact that will reach far beyond that range.

NEW FRONTIERS AWAIT

Expectations about workspace design are also being set on campuses that foster entrepreneurship within their student populations. Some institutions provide physical space for their "incubators" that is completely modular, allowing interdisciplinary project teams to draw upon diverse talents across the university. Successful entrepreneurs will model their company's workspace on those environments, and team members will seek out companies that foster a similar work dynamic.

UNCHARTED TERRITORY AWAITS THE FACILITIES MANAGER. AT iOFFICE, WE ARE SADDLED UP. WE HOPE YOU WILL RIDE WITH US, AS CUSTOMERS AND STRATEGIC PARTNERS, INTO THE WIDE OPEN WORKSPACE.

Uncharted territory awaits the Facilities Manager. At iOffice, we are saddled up. We hope you will ride with us, as customers and strategic partners, into the Wide Open Workspace.

VOICE OF THE CUSTOMER

WORKSPACE AS A TALENT MAGNET

We talked with some of our customers about the role that workspace plays in attracting and retaining talent. Three customers representing very different industries reinforced the importance of space as a competitive factor.

A DIFFERENTIATOR. "Every group in our company is focused on hiring and retaining talent, the C-suite even more so. The workplace can be a differentiator in hiring, retaining talent, and for increasing employee productivity."

A MAGNET. "It's all about retention and recruiting. Trying to attract the best talent to our organization is paramount to our business, because everybody's after that same talent pool. So what makes us different? Today, we have our own building and we have location. We have amenities, all the way down to the furniture and fixtures. Nobody else in town can say they have what we have. So when we are recruiting, we want that talent to come in and look for themselves. We host all kinds of events to bring recruits in to see the space. Their reactions? 'This is really nice.' 'I like the artwork.' 'This is classy.'"

A SOURCE OF PRIDE. "Companies must provide high-quality workspaces in order to retain and attract the best talent. The spaces must be designed in a fashion that provides a combination of open and common spaces for impromptu meetings along with heads-down spaces with a feel of openness. Workers must have access to quality furniture; in many cases this includes ergonomic features with sit-to-stand options. Lots of glass, good sound-masking equipment, and attractive architecture all play a role in creating superior workspaces. Daylight harvesting, solar power, LEED, recycling, and other programs that promote the responsible use of resources give employees a sense of pride because the company they work for is a responsible corporate citizen."

ACKNOWLEDGMENTS

FIRST, WE WOULD LIKE to thank all of the iOffice employees. Without such an amazing team we would not be able to successfully create such amazing products nor effectively serve our customers. They make coming to work exciting and fun!

We would also like to thank our partners, contractors, and vendors for their support and exceptional services.

Finally, we want to acknowledge the generous amount of love and support we receive from our family and friends. Without these folks, we would have been hard pressed to persevere. They are the force that sustains us, encouraging us in the challenging times and rejoicing when success is achieved!

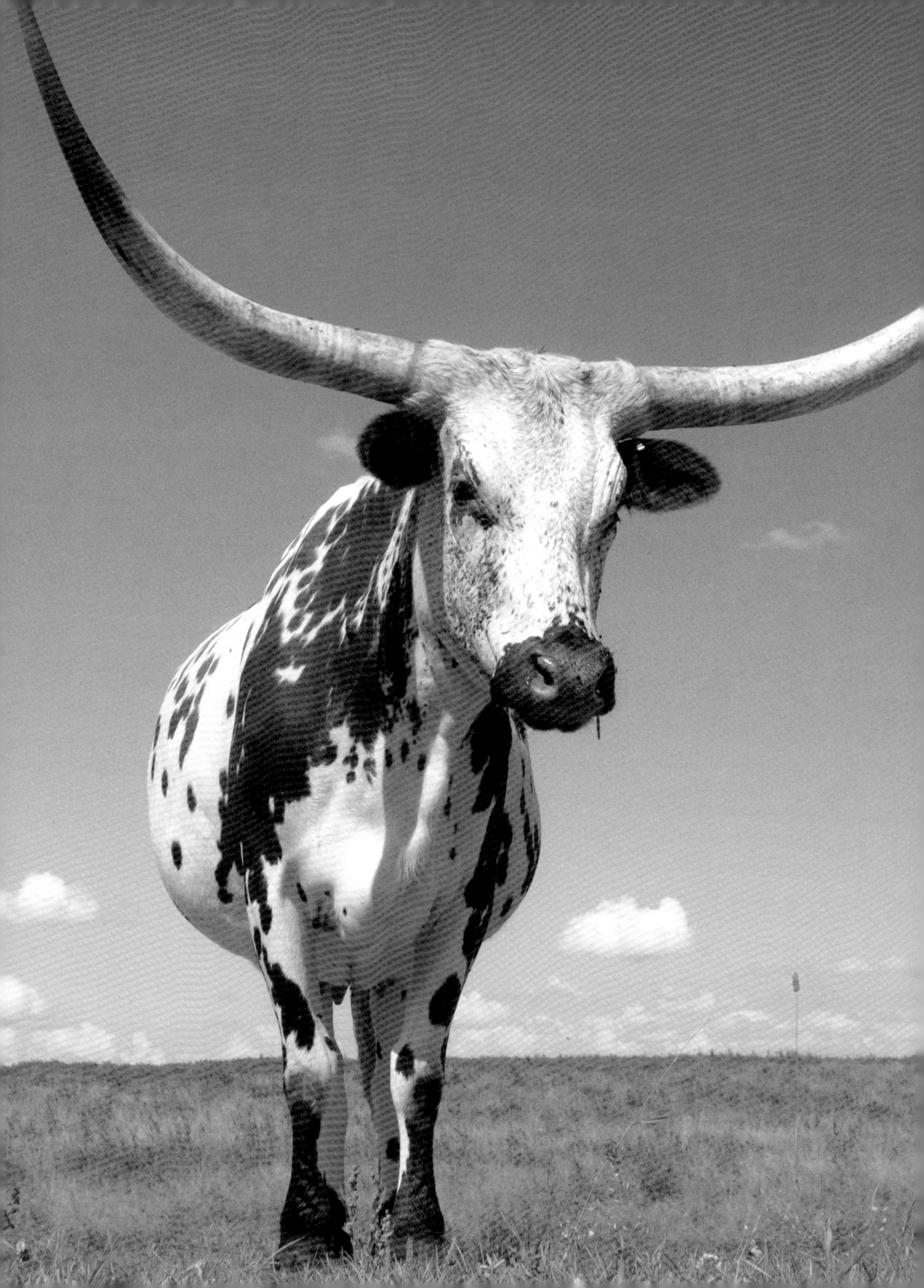

BIBLIOGRAPHY

"7-Eleven, Inc. History." *FundingUniverse.* Accessed December 14, 2013. http://www.fundinguniverse.com/company-histories/7-eleven-inc-history/.

Barker, Eugene C. "Stephen Fuller Austin: The Father of Texas (1793–1836)." *Texas A&M University.* Accessed September 12, 2013. http://www.tamu.edu/faculty/ccbn/dewitt/adp/history/bios/austin/austin.html.

"The Birth of the Microchip." *Longview Institute.* Accessed September 13, 2013. http://www.longviewinstitute.org/projects/marketfundamentalism/microchip.

"Blake Mycoskie." *TheHuffingtonPost.com.* Accessed September 10, 2013. http://www.huffingtonpost.com/blake-mycoskie/.

"Blake Mycoskie." *TOMS.* Accessed September 10, 2013. http://www.toms.com/blakes-bio/l.

"Carrie Marcus Neiman: Businesswoman, 1883–1953." *The University of Texas at Austin: Great Texas Women.* Accessed September 12, 2013. http://www.utexas.edu/gtw/neiman.php.

Chapman, Betty T. "Ella Fondren Played Pivotal Role in City's Progress." *Houston Business Journal* (August 3, 2008). http://www.bizjournals.com/houston/stories/2008/08/04/story15.html?page=all.

"Chisholm Trail." *Wikipedia.* Accessed September 11, 2013. http://en.wikipedia.org/wiki/Chisholm_Trail.

Cowen, Tyler. "Why Texas Is Our Future." *Time Magazine* (October 28, 2013). http://content.time.com/time/magazine/article/0,9171,2154995,00.html#ixzz2jnmTfHkG.

DeMoss, Dorothy D. "Neiman, Carrie Marcus." *Texas State Historical Association: The Handbook of Texas.* Accessed September 13, 2013. http://www.tshaonline.org/handbook/online/articles/fne30.

Earnest, Martha, and Melvin Sance. "Wallace, Daniel Webster." *Texas State Historical Association: The Handbook of Texas.* Accessed September 10, 2013. http://www.tshaonline.org/handbook/online/articles/fwaah.

Goldenberg, Suzanne. "US Surpasses Russia as World's Top Oil and Natural Gas Producer." *The Guardian* (October 4, 2013). http://www.theguardian.com/business/2013/oct/04/us-oil-natural-gas-production-russia-saudi-arabia.

Gores, Paul. "Overseeing a Change of Fortune at Associated Bank." *Milwaukee-Wisconsin Journal Sentinel* (November 9, 2013). http://www.jsonline.com/business/overseeing-a-change-of-fortune-at-associated-bank-b99136822z1-231300621.html.

Grieder, Erica. *Big, Hot, Cheap, and Right: What America Can Learn from the Strange Genius of Texas.* New York: PublicAffairs, 2013.

Hardy, Quentin. "In Battle Over Dell, a Founder Hopes to Reclaim His Legacy." *The New York Times* (July 14, 2013). http://www.nytimes.com/2013/07/15/technology/in-dell-battle-a-founder-hopes-to-reclaim-his-legacy.html?pagewanted=all&_r=0.

"Henrietta King: Rancher, 1832–1925." *The University of Texas at Austin: Great Texas Women.* Accessed September 11, 2013. http://www.utexas.edu/gtw/king.php.

"History." *7-Eleven.* Accessed December 14, 2013. http://corp.7-eleven.com/AboutUs/History/tabid/75/Default.aspx.

"The History of Cowboy Boots." *CowboyBoots.com.* Accessed September 11, 2013. http://www.cowboyboots.com/history.html.

"History and Traditions." *The University of Texas at Austin.* Accessed September 10, 2013. https://www.utexas.edu/about-ut/history-traditions.

BIBLIOGRAPHY

"Jack S. Kilby - Biographical." *Nobelprize.org*. Accessed September 10, 2013. http://www.nobelprize.org/nobel_prizes/physics/laureates/2000/kilby-bio.html.

Jasinski, Laurie E. "South by Southwest." *Texas State Historical Association: The Handbook of Texas*. Accessed September 10, 2013. http://www.tshaonline.org/handbook/online/articles/xfsfr.

"Jesse Chisholm." *Wikipedia*. Accessed September 11, 2013. http://en.wikipedia.org/wiki/Jesse_Chisholm.

Kleiner, Diana J. "Fondren, Walter William." *Texas State Historical Association: The Handbook of Texas*. Accessed September 19, 2013. http://www.tshaonline.org/handbook/online/articles/ffo29.

Kreneck, Thomas H. "Houston, Samuel." *Texas State Historical Association: The Handbook of Texas*. Accessed September 10, 2013. http://www.tshaonline.org/handbook/online/articles/fho73.

Martin, Douglas. "George Mitchell, a Pioneer in Hydraulic Fracturing, Dies at 94." *The New York Times* (July 26, 2013). http://www.nytimes.com/2013/07/27/business/george-mitchell-a-pioneer-in-hydraulic-fracturing-dies-at-94.html?pagewanted=all&_r=3&.

"Mary Kay Ash." *American National Biography Online*. Accessed September 11, 2013. http://www.anb.org/articles/10/10-02284.html.

"Michael Dell." *The Biography Channel*. Accessed Dec 17, 2013. http://www.biography.com/people/michael-dell-9542199.

Mouawad, Jad. "Pushing 40, Southwest Is Still Playing the Rebel." *The New York Times* (November 20, 2010). http://www.nytimes.com/2010/11/21/business/21south.html?pagewanted=all&_r=0.

"History." *South by Southwest*. Accessed September 10, 2013. http://sxsw.com/music/history.

"Our Story." *Half Price Books*. Accessed September 10, 2013. http://hpb.com/about/.

Owen, James P., and David R. Stoecklein. *Cowboy Ethics: What Wall Street Can Learn from the Code of the West*. Ketchum, ID: Stoecklein Publishing, 2004.

Robb, Walter, and A. C. Gallo. "GMO Labeling Coming to Whole Foods Market." *Whole Story: The Official Whole Foods Market® Blog.* Accessed September 14, 2013. http://www.wholefoodsmarket.com /blog/gmo-labeling-coming-whole-foods-market?utm_medium=Any _Social_Media&utm_source=SocialMedia&utm_campaign=GMO _Labeling&sf10261252=1.

"Roundups." *Ask.com.* Accessed October 11, 2013. http://www.ask .com/wikiCowboy?o=2801&qsrc=999&ad=doubleDown&an =apn&ap=ask.com#Roundups.

Sneed, Edgar P. "King, Henrietta Chamberlain." *Texas State Historical Association: The Handbook of Texas.* Accessed September 10, 2013. http://www.tshaonline.org/handbook/online/articles/fki16.

"South by Southwest." *Wikipedia.* Accessed September 11, 2013. http://en.wikipedia.org/wiki/South_by_Southwest.

"Spoetzl Brewery." *Wikipedia.* Accessed September 11, 2013. http:// en.wikipedia.org/wiki/Spoetzl_Brewery.

Sustainable Brands. "Sustainable Business Transformation Through Workspace Innovation Summary." *Scribd.* Accessed December 18, 2013. http://www.scribd.com/doc/61566695/Sustainable-Business -Transformation-Through-Workspace-Innovation-Summary.

"Timeline: UT History from 1883 to the Present." *UT History Central.* Accessed September 10, 2013. http://www.texasexes.org/uthistory /timeline.aspx.

"United States Small Business Friendliness: 2013 Thumbtack. com Small Business Survey, in Partnership with the Kauffman Foundation." *Thumbtack.* http://www.thumbtack.com/survey#2013 /cities.

"What's Behind the Acme Name." *Acme Brick Company.* Accessed September 10, 2013. http://www.brick.com/aboutus/acmename.htm.

Wyly, Sam, and Andrew Wyly. *Texas Got It Right!* New York: Melcher, 2012.

Zanetell, Myrna. "Tony Lama Company." *Texas State Historical Association: The Handbook of Texas.* Accessed September 11, 2013. http://www.tshaonline.org/handbook/online/articles/dlt01.

INDEX

A

Acme Brick Company, 70
Airline Deregulation Act, 21
Alvarez, Carlos, 46
Ash, Mary Kay, 42–43
Associated Bank, 83
Austin, Moses, 97, 126
Austin, Stephen, 97, 126

B

balanced scorecard, 128, 130
Barbaro, Nick, 112
barcode scanning, 76
beer brewing industry, 46
benchmarks, 55, 128, 130. *See also* metrics
Black, Louis, 112
blazing new trails. *See also* Flexspace (Sabre Holdings)
    about, 17–19
    Jesse Chisholm, 18, 24
    at iOffice, 31
    tools for, 30–31, 33
bonds, forming, 107
booksellers, 131
brand loyalty. *See* loyalty (riding for the brand)

C

campfire metaphor. *See* sharing around the campfire

cattle business, 114
cell phone technology, 119
change/change management
    challenges of, 23
    forces driving, 15
    skills for, 132
    tools for seamless transitions, 41, 44, 47, 49
    validation through employees for, 58
    of workspace configuration, 25–26
Chisholm, Jesse, 18, 24
Chisholm Trail, 5, 18, 24
chores
    iOffice tools for managing, 78
    of relocation, 74–75
    tackling, 71–72
    taking pride in doing, 39, 65–66, 87
    in workplace management, 66, 69
Cigarroa, Francisco G., 48, 136
Clinton, Bill, 125
cloud computing
    accessing documents in the cloud, 76
    cloud-based software, 33, 41, 77
code of honor, 4, 11, 121
collaboration. *See also* roundups
    for achieving collaboration, 45
    examples of, 39, 41, 42–43, 44, 46
    focus/emphasis on, 15
    for innovation, 116–117
    by iOffice, 118
    metrics for, 58
    University of Texas system for, 48

communication. *See* sharing around the campfire
conflict resolution, 95
corporate citizenship, 15
corporate culture
    collaboration and rapport, 110
    Mary Kay Cosmetics, 43
    sharing (*See* sharing around the campfire)
    Southwest Airlines, 21, 123
Corporate & Facilities Services Representatives, 14
corporate responsibility, 125
corporate values, 11, 21, 43
corporate vision
    Francisco Cigarroa's, 48, 136
    Michael Dell's, 29
    iOffice, 2
    long-term, 128, 132
    TOMS, 125
costs
    of creating office space, 84
    efficiency in reducing, 83
    loss of customers, 99
    of moving, 72
    operating, 1
    reduction of, 20, 130
courage
    Sam Houston's story, 53
    iOffice platform and, 59–60
    for looking beyond walls, 62
    metrics for bolstering, 58
    ten-gallon hat metaphor, 51–52
    in workspace arena, 54
cowboy boots, 89
cowboy code. *See also* Workspace Cowboys
    about, 11, 13
    blazing new trails (*See* blazing new trails)
    courage (*See* courage)
    getting together for the roundup (*See* roundups)
    keeping it simple (*See* simplicity)
    riding for the brand (*See* loyalty (riding for the brand))
    sharing (*See* sharing around the campfire)
    taking pride in chores (*See* pride)
    trust (*See* trust)
cowboys, as inspiration, 4–5
Cowen, Tyler, 136
cowgirls, 11, 61
C-suite, 34, 58, 138
cubicle walls, managing changes to, 33–35
culture. *See* corporate culture
customers, success of, 133

D

Dell, Michael, 19, 28–29
Dell Computer Corporation, 29
design of workspace
    for collaboration, 45
    LEED (Leadership in Energy and Environmental Design) certification, 8, 15, 44, 46
    for mobility, 90
    new rules for, 34–35
    occupancy during redesign/changes, 47
    simplicity in, 91
    for space utilization, 20
    for university campuses, 137
    using iOffice, 74–75

E

efficiency, 83, 99–100, 102
employees/workforce. *See also* mobility
    adaptability of, 23
    attracting talented, 2, 109, 116, 138
    expectations of, 2, 15
    generational shift in workforce, 15
    participation in change by, 26
    plans for moving, 47, 49
    taking care of, 61
    validation through voices of, 58
energy industry, 56–57, 75, 77–78
environment, work. *See* corporate culture; workspace/office space
environmental responsibility, 15, 57
eyewear (TOMS), 125

F

Facilities Managers
    about, 4
    budget management by, 69
    challenges for, 51
    courage of, 52, 54
    duties of, 8, 10, 14
    planning for workspace changes, 38
    responsibilities of, 6

INDEX

Facilities Teams
   about, 14
   duties of, 39, 41
   pride in, 67
   responsibilities of, 6, 8
   roles of, 45
flexspace. *See also* workspace/
     office space
   description and origin of, 19–20
   management of, in healthcare
     environment, 117
   switching to, 22–23, 62
   using and tracking, 30
Flexspace (Sabre Holdings), 19, 113,
   124, 127, 130, 132. *See also*
   Sabre Holdings
Flynn, Philip, 83
Fondren, Walter and Ella, 68
footwear (TOMS), 125
footwear of cowboys, 89
Fortune 500 companies, 15
Fortune magazine, 125
Foursquare, 112
fracking, 57

G

gas industry, 54, 56–57, 59
gender neutrality, 11
generational shift in workforce,
   15, 108–109
Generation Y, 109
getting together for roundups.
   See roundups
GMO labeling, 98
Golden Rule, 43
Goodnight, Charles, 95–96
Goodnight-Loving Trail, 96
Green, John Jefferson, 86
green initiatives, 2, 8
The Guardian, 57

H

Half Price Books, 131
Harvard Business School, 135
healthcare industry
   iOffice modules for, 22–23, 75,
     87–88, 101, 117

honor, code of, 4, 11, 121
hoteling, 20, 22, 128
Houston, Sam, 53

I

ice boxes, 86
Idea Community, 118
identity theft, 108–109
Ikard, Bose, 96
innovations
   mail delivery, 113, 115
   microchips, 119
   mindset of iOffice for, 116–118
   of Workspace Cowboys, 118
iOffice (company)
   blazing trails at, 31, 33
   innovation mindset of, 116–118
   riding for the brand and, 133
iOffice platform
   building trust with, 101
   courage for implementing, 59–60
   functions of (gas company
     example), 55, 59
   for healthcare industry, 22–23, 75,
     87–88, 101, 117
   Mail Module, 115
   purpose and uses of, 3–4
   relocation tools, 74–75
   SaaS (software as a service)
     solution, 99–100, 102
   simplicity of, 88
   Space Management Module, 39,
     71–72
   tracking tools, 77–78
   workspace management with,
     3–4, 78

K

keeping it simple. *See* simplicity
Kelleher, Herb, 21
Kilby, Jack S., 119
King, Henrietta Chamberlain, 61
King, Richard, 61
kiosk-based service delivery, 109,
   115, 117
Kleberg, Robert Justus, 61
knowledge workers, 10

147

L

leadership, 122
LEED (Leadership in Energy and Environmental Design) certification, 8, 15, 44, 46, 127
leveraging technology, 122
Loving, Oliver, 95–96
loyalty (riding for the brand)
    attracting loyal employees, 124
    championing workspace for, 127
    cowboy code of honor, 11, 121
    iOffice and, 133
    TOMS shoes, 125
    Whole Foods Market, 123

M

mail delivery innovations, 113, 115
Mallet, John W., 48
managed document services (MDS), 117
Martinez, Antonio Maria, 97
Mary Kay Cosmetics, 42–43
Masters of Business Administration (MBA) programs, 135
MBA (Masters of Business Administration) programs, 135
MDS (managed document services), 117
metrics, 58, 128, 132. *See also* benchmarks
Meyers, Louis, 112
microbrewing company, collaboration in, 46
Millennials, 15, 109, 123
Mitchell, George, 56–57
mobility
    adapting to, 20
    benefits of, 2, 15
    designing workspace for, 90
    iOffice support for, 30–31
    promoting, 22
    reconfiguring space for, 25
    tools for, 1, 108
mock trials, 38
moving/relocation, 47, 49, 71–72, 74–75
Mycoskie, Blake, 125

N

Neiman, Carrie Marcus, 104
Neiman Marcus, 104
Non-GMO Project, 98

O

office space. *See* workspace/office space
offsite workforce, tools for, 30–31
oil industry, 56–57, 66, 68
One for One idea, 125
open range metaphor, 4–5
OpenSpace, 91, 117
operating costs, 1

P

paperless office, 76, 99
performance
    defining and measuring, 128, 130
    investment in technology for, 15
Petzold, Oswald, 46
Presidential Medal of Freedom, 57
pride
    in chores, 39, 65–66, 87
    in Facilities Teams, 67
    sources of, 138
problem solving, collaboration for, 45
productivity
    consideration for workspace neighbors, 34
    smaller footprint and expenditures, 15
    through mobility, 2
    through sharing knowledge, 110

R

real estate assets, 1–2. *See also* workspace/office space
relocation/moving
    finding simple solutions for, 85, 87
    iOffice services and, 71–72, 74–75
    travel offices, 90
reports, generation of real-time, 100, 102
restacking, 39, 41

INDEX

retail industry, 39, 41, 44, 69, 71–72, 104, 131
return on investment (ROI), 58
riding for the brand. *See* loyalty (riding for the brand)
rodeo metaphor, 40
roughnecks, 19, 56–57
roundups, 37–38, 40, 44, 48. *See also* collaboration; teamwork

S

SaaS (software as a service) solution, 99, 117
Sabre Holdings, 19, 113
    Flexspace, 124, 127, 130, 132
    loyalty (riding for the brand), 124, 127–128
service delivery, 47, 49, 59, 100, 101, 102, 105
    mail delivery innovation, 113, 115
7-Eleven, 86
sharing around the campfire, 30–31, 107
    higher education innovation through, 113, 115
    tools for, 113
    use of iOffice in, 116–118
    use of technology and, 108–109
    in the workspace arena, 110
sharing space, 20, 22
Shiner Brewing Association, 46
simplicity
    cowboy metaphor for, 81
    iOffice's approach to design with, 88, 91, 93
    of tools, 82, 85, 93
site inspections, 117
social media, 109, 110, 112
soft rules
    behavior in new workspaces, 26, 30
    for office space design, 34–35
software as a service (SaaS) solution, 99, 117
South by Southwest (SXSW), 112
Southland Ice Company, 86
Southwest Airlines, 19, 21, 123
space management. *See* workspace/office space
Spindletop oilfield, 68

Spoetzl, Kosmos, 46
standards, external, 58
State of Texas. *See* Texas
strategic partnership, 127
students
    mail delivery innovation for, 113, 115
    use of technology by, 108–109
success of customers, 133
Swenson, Roland, 112
SXSW (South by Southwest), 112
systems consolidation, 100

T

talent. *See* employees/workforce
teamwork. *See also* collaboration
    centralization of teams, 75, 77–78
    enhancement of, through collaboration, 45, 46
    Facilities Representative, 38
    location/relocation of teams, 84
    tackling chores, 69, 71–72
technology
    changes in software development and installation, 31, 33
    cloud-based software, 41
    dependency on, 108–109
    for leadership, 122
    Texas Instruments' innovations in, 119
ten-gallon hat metaphor. *See* courage
Texas
    Chisholm Trail, 5, 18, 24
    establishment of, 97, 126
    history of, 136
    "The United States of Texas: Why the Lone Star State Is America's Future" (Cowen), 136
    University of Texas, 28, 29, 48, 136
Texas Instruments (TI), 119
Thompson, Joe C., Jr., 86
Thumbtack survey, 123
Time magazine, 136
TOMS footwear and eyewear, 125
tools
    cowboy metaphor for choosing, 81
    for creating and supporting trust, 102
    finding what works, 82, 85, 87

149

tools *(continued)*
    for improving efficiency, 99–100, 102
    for managing chores, 78
    need for simplicity of, 93
    for offsite workforce, 30–31
    relocation, 74–75
    for seamless transitions, 41, 44, 47, 49
    for sharing, 113
    simplicity of, 93
    tracking, 77–78
touchdown space, 90
tracking tools, 77–78
trailblazing. *See* **blazing new trails**
transformable spaces, 128, 130
transition tools, 41, 44, 47, 49
transparency, 98
travel industry, 19, 21. *See also* **Sabre Holdings**
travel offices, 90
trends
    dealing with space, 135
    environmental responsibility, 15
    paperless office, 76
    social media, 109
trust
    among cowboys, 95–96
    through service delivery, 104
    tools for creating and supporting, 102
    transparency for, 98
    between vendors and customers, 100, 101
    in workspace arena, 96, 99–100, 105

U

"The United States of Texas: Why the Lone Star State Is America's Future" (Cowen), 136
University of Texas, 28, 29, 48, 136
unsung heroes, 54, 60, 69
used book sellers, 131

V

value enhancement, 100, 132
values, 11, 21, 43
vision. *See* **corporate vision**

W

Wallace, Daniel Webster, 114
Wayne, John, 11
Whole Foods Market, 98, 123
wide open mind, 110
Wide Open Workspace (WOW)
    about the movement, 2, 4
    customer success and, 133
    productivity and, 110
    technology for, 122
    transitioning to, 33
Woodlands, Texas community, 57
workforce. *See* **employees/workforce**
Workspace Cowboys. *See also* **cowboy code**
    about, 2
    being considerate of your neighbors, 34
    brand loyalty of, 124
    change management by, 132
    as facilitators for collaboration, 38–39
    gender neutrality and, 11
    innovations of, 118
    mindset of, 10, 128
    problem solving methods of, 33
    strategic partnerships of, 127
    successful, 130
    tasks and responsibilities of, 5–11
    as unsung heroes, 54, 60, 69
workspace/office space. *See also* **design of workspace; flexspace**
    adaptability to new office environments, 23
    assigned, 22
    attention to environment, 25–26
    attractiveness of, 59–60
    changing cubicle walls, 33–35
    chores in management of, 66, 69
    consideration for neighbors in, 34
    costs of creating, 84
    courage in workspace arena, 52, 54
    evolution of, 15, 122
    hoteling, 20, 22, 128
    for housing teams, 84
    iOffice Space Management Module, 39, 117
    mobility and configuration of, 25–26, 90 (*See also* mobility)
    planning for changes to, 38

INDEX

as real estate, 1–2
reorganization of facilities, 75, 77–78
seeking new locations for, 62
sharing space, 20, 22
soft rules for behavior in, 26, 30, 34–35
strategic utilization of, 122
as talent magnet, 116, 138
transformable, 128, 130
utilization of, 87–88
workspace challenge for iOffice, 3–4

WOW. *See* **Wide Open Workspace (WOW)**

Y

Yergin, Daniel, 57

Z

Zuckerberg, Mark, 112

WIDE OPEN WORKSPACE

www.WideOpenWorkspace.com